Super BIBLE PICTURE FUN FOR KIDS

Bible Picture Fun © 2001 by Barbour Publishing, Inc.
Bible Connect the Dots © 2001 by Barbour Publishing, Inc.

Super Bible Picture Fun for Kids © 2009 by Barbour Publishing, Inc.

ISBN 978-1-60260-395-0

Published by Barbour Publishing, Inc., P.O. Box 719, Uhrichsville, Ohio 44683, www.barbourbooks.com

Our mission is to publish and distribute inspirational products offering exceptional value and biblical encouragement to the masses.

Member of the
Evangelical Christian
Publishers Association

Printed in the United States of America.

Super
BIBLE
PICTURE FUN
FOR
KIDS

BARBOUR
PUBLISHING

COLOR THE PICTURE

CREATURES OF THE BIBLE

JUST FOR FUN, LET'S HAVE A LOOK AT THE *CREATURES OF THE BIBLE*. FROM ANIMALS TO INSECTS, TO CREATURES THAT SWIM IN THE SEA OR SLITHER ON THE GROUND, THE WORD OF GOD JUST ABOUT COVERS THEM ALL.

WE WILL SEE THAT ANIMALS WERE AN IMPORTANT PART OF PEOPLE'S LIVES BACK IN THE TIME THAT THE BOOKS OF THE BIBLE WERE WRITTEN.

MANY TIMES, WE WILL FIND THAT THE BIBLE EVEN COMPARES *US* TO ANIMALS AS IT TRIES TO HELP US DISCOVER TRUTHS ABOUT OURSELVES.

WHO KNOWS? WE MIGHT EVEN DISCOVER ANIMALS THAT ARE STRANGE OR UNKNOWN TO US TODAY.

ENJOY!

FiNiSH *the* PiCTURE

ON THE FOLLOWING PAGE, USE THE GRID TO
COMPLETE THE PICTURE BY DUPLICATING THE
FINISHED HALF ONTO THE UNFINISHED AREA.

"THE LORD HARDENED THE HEART
OF PHARAOH KING OF EGYPT, SO THAT
HE PURSUED THE ISRAELITES, WHO
WERE MARCHING OUT BOLDLY. THE
EGYPTIANS—ALL PHARAOH'S *HORSES*
AND CHARIOTS, HORSEMEN AND
TROOPS—PURSUED THE ISRAELITES
AND OVERTOOK THEM AS THEY CAMPED
BY THE SEA NEAR PI HAHIROTH,
OPPOSITE BAAL ZEPHON."

EXODUS 14:8–9

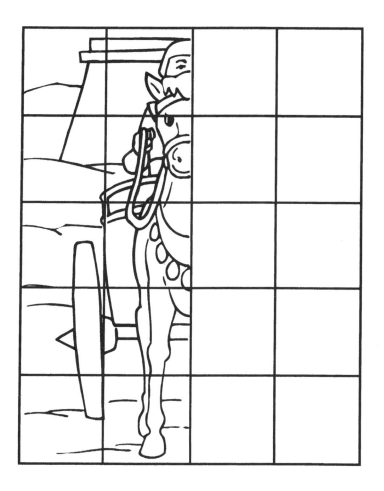

7

FiNiSH *the* PiCTURE

USING THE GRID, DRAW THE PICTURE BELOW ON THE FOLLOWING PAGE.

READY TO RUN!

PiCTURE PiECES

PUT THE PICTURE PIECES IN THE RIGHT ORDER.
DRAW WHAT IS IN EACH NUMBERED BOX
BELOW INTO EACH BOX OF THE SAME NUMBER
ON THE FOLLOWING PAGE.

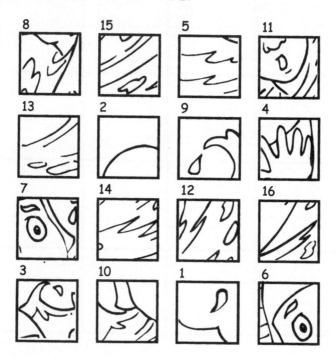

1	2	3	4
5	6	7	8
9	10	11	12
13	14	15	16

"WHEN PHARAOH'S *HORSES*, CHARIOTS AND HORSEMEN WENT INTO THE SEA, THE LORD BROUGHT THE WATERS OF THE SEA BACK OVER THEM, BUT THE ISRAELITES WALKED THROUGH THE SEA ON DRY GROUND."

EXODUS 15:19

MISSING PIECES

DOES THE PICTURE ON THE NEXT PAGE LOOK A LITTLE UNFINISHED TO YOU? A LOT OF THINGS ARE LEFT OUT, BUT YOU CAN FINISH IT BY FILLING IN AS MANY MISSING PIECES AS YOU CAN FIND. LOOK CAREFULLY!

"THEY CAME OUT WITH ALL THEIR TROOPS AND A LARGE NUMBER OF *HORSES* AND CHARIOTS—A HUGE ARMY, AS NUMEROUS AS THE SAND ON THE SEASHORE. ALL THESE KINGS JOINED FORCES AND MADE CAMP TOGETHER AT THE WATERS OF MEROM, TO FIGHT AGAINST ISRAEL."

JOSHUA 11:4–5

WHAT'S DIFFERENT?

LOOK CAREFULLY AT THE PICTURE BELOW AND THE ONE ON THE NEXT PAGE. THEY LOOK THE SAME AT FIRST GLANCE, BUT. . .ARE THEY? CIRCLE ANY DIFFERENCES YOU FIND.

"IN THE COURSE OF TIME, ABSALOM PROVIDED HIMSELF WITH A CHARIOT AND *HORSES* AND WITH FIFTY MEN TO RUN AHEAD OF HIM."

2 SAMUEL 15:1

HIDDEN LETTERS

ON THE NEXT PAGE, COLOR IN THE AREAS THAT CONTAIN A SQUARE TO REVEAL THE HIDDEN LETTERS. THEN USE THE LETTERS TO COMPLETE THE VERSE BELOW.

"AS THEY WERE WALKING ALONG AND TALKING TOGETHER, SUDDENLY A CHARIOT OF FIRE AND __ __ __ __ __ __ OF FIRE APPEARED AND SEPARATED THE TWO OF THEM, AND ELIJAH WENT UP TO HEAVEN IN A WHIRLWIND."

2 KINGS 2:11

_ _ _ _ _ _ _

FiNiSH the PiCTURE

USING THE GRID, DRAW THE PICTURE BELOW ON THE FOLLOWING PAGE.

FLEECE AS WHITE AS SNOW

COLOR THE PICTURE

"THERE HE SAW A WELL IN THE FIELD, WITH THREE FLOCKS OF *SHEEP* LYING NEAR IT BECAUSE THE FLOCKS WERE WATERED FROM THAT WELL. THE STONE OVER THE MOUTH OF THE WELL WAS LARGE."

GENESIS 29:2

PiCTURE PiECES

PUT THE PICTURE PIECES IN THE RIGHT ORDER.
DRAW WHAT IS IN EACH NUMBERED BOX
BELOW INTO EACH BOX OF THE SAME NUMBER
ON THE FOLLOWING PAGE.

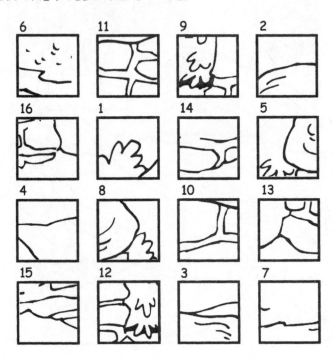

1	2	3	4
5	6	7	8
9	10	11	12
13	14	15	16

"WHEN ALL THE FLOCKS WERE GATHERED THERE, THE SHEPHERDS WOULD ROLL THE STONE AWAY FROM THE WELL'S MOUTH AND WATER THE *SHEEP*. THEN THEY WOULD RETURN THE STONE TO ITS PLACE OVER THE MOUTH OF THE WELL."

GENESIS 29:3

WHAT'S DIFFERENT?

LOOK CAREFULLY AT THE PICTURE BELOW AND THE ONE ON THE NEXT PAGE. THEY LOOK THE SAME AT FIRST GLANCE, BUT. . .ARE THEY? CIRCLE ANY DIFFERENCES YOU FIND.

"WHILE HE WAS STILL TALKING WITH THEM, RACHEL CAME WITH HER FATHER'S *SHEEP*, FOR SHE WAS A SHEPHERDESS."

GENESIS 29:9

FiNiSH the PiCTURE

ON THE FOLLOWING PAGE, USE THE GRID TO
COMPLETE THE PICTURE BY DUPLICATING THE
FINISHED HALF ONTO THE UNFINISHED AREA.

"'LET ME GO THROUGH ALL YOUR
FLOCKS TODAY AND REMOVE FROM
THEM EVERY SPECKLED OR SPOTTED
SHEEP, EVERY DARK-COLORED LAMB
AND EVERY SPOTTED OR SPECKLED
GOAT. THEY WILL BE MY WAGES.'"

GENESIS 30:32

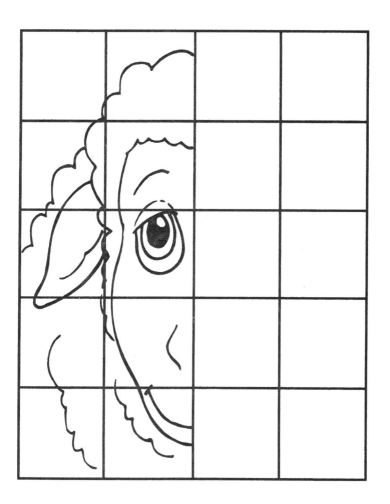

MISSING PIECES

DOES THE PICTURE ON THE NEXT PAGE LOOK A LITTLE UNFINISHED TO YOU? A LOT OF THINGS ARE LEFT OUT, BUT YOU CAN FINISH IT BY FILLING IN AS MANY MISSING PIECES AS YOU CAN FIND. LOOK CAREFULLY!

"DAVID SAID TO GOD, 'WAS IT NOT I WHO ORDERED THE FIGHTING MEN TO BE COUNTED? I AM THE ONE WHO HAS SINNED AND DONE WRONG. THESE ARE BUT *SHEEP*. WHAT HAVE THEY DONE? O LORD MY GOD, LET YOUR HAND FALL UPON ME AND MY FAMILY, BUT DO NOT LET THIS PLAGUE REMAIN ON YOUR PEOPLE.'"

1 CHRONICLES 21:17

HIDDEN LETTERS

ON THE NEXT PAGE, COLOR IN THE AREAS THAT
CONTAIN A SQUARE TO REVEAL THE HIDDEN
LETTERS. THEN USE THE LETTERS TO COMPLETE
THE VERSE BELOW.

"BUT HE BROUGHT HIS PEOPLE OUT
    LIKE A FLOCK;
  HE LED THEM LIKE __ __ __ __ __
    THROUGH THE DESERT.
HE GUIDED THEM SAFELY, SO THEY
    WERE UNAFRAID;
  BUT THE SEA ENGULFED THEIR
    ENEMIES."

PSALM 78:52–53

_ _ _ _ _ _ _

FINISH the PICTURE

USING THE GRID, DRAW THE PICTURE BELOW
ON THE FOLLOWING PAGE.

BILLY IS HIS NAME

PiCTURE PiECES

PUT THE PICTURE PIECES IN THE RIGHT ORDER.
DRAW WHAT IS IN EACH NUMBERED BOX
BELOW INTO EACH BOX OF THE SAME NUMBER
ON THE FOLLOWING PAGE.

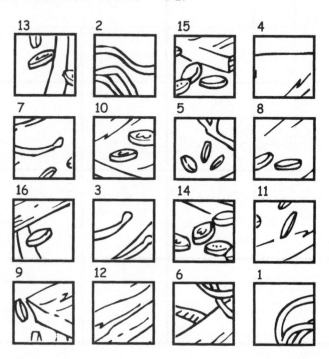

1	2	3	4
5	6	7	8
9	10	11	12
13	14	15	16

"SO HE MADE A WHIP OUT OF CORDS, AND DROVE ALL FROM THE TEMPLE AREA, BOTH *SHEEP* AND CATTLE; HE SCATTERED THE COINS OF THE MONEY CHANGERS AND OVERTURNED THEIR TABLES."

JOHN 2:15

MISSING PIECES

DOES THE PICTURE ON THE NEXT PAGE LOOK A LITTLE UNFINISHED TO YOU? A LOT OF THINGS ARE LEFT OUT, BUT YOU CAN FINISH IT BY FILLING IN AS MANY MISSING PIECES AS YOU CAN FIND. LOOK CAREFULLY!

"'I HAVE OTHER *SHEEP* THAT ARE NOT OF THIS SHEEP PEN. I MUST BRING THEM ALSO. THEY TOO WILL LISTEN TO MY VOICE, AND THERE SHALL BE ONE FLOCK AND ONE SHEPHERD.'"

JOHN 10:16

COLOR THE PICTURE

"HE HAD THE *CAMELS* KNEEL DOWN NEAR THE WELL OUTSIDE THE TOWN; IT WAS TOWARD EVENING, THE TIME THE WOMEN GO OUT TO DRAW WATER."

GENESIS 24:11

WHAT'S DIFFERENT?

LOOK CAREFULLY AT THE PICTURE BELOW AND
THE ONE ON THE NEXT PAGE. THEY LOOK
THE SAME AT FIRST GLANCE, BUT. . .ARE THEY?
CIRCLE ANY DIFFERENCES YOU FIND.

"HERDS OF *CAMELS* WILL COVER YOUR LAND, YOUNG CAMELS OF MIDIAN AND EPHAH. AND ALL FROM SHEBA WILL COME, BEARING GOLD AND INCENSE AND PROCLAIMING THE PRAISE OF THE LORD."

ISAIAH 60:6

FiNiSH *the* PiCTURE

ON THE FOLLOWING PAGE, USE THE GRID TO
COMPLETE THE PICTURE BY DUPLICATING THE
FINISHED HALF ONTO THE UNFINISHED AREA.

"SO THE MAN WENT TO THE HOUSE,
AND THE *CAMELS* WERE UNLOADED.
STRAW AND FODDER WERE BROUGHT
FOR THE CAMELS, AND WATER FOR HIM
AND HIS MEN TO WASH THEIR FEET."

GENESIS 24:32

COLOR the PICTURE

"WHEN TWO FULL YEARS HAD PASSED, PHARAOH HAD A DREAM: HE WAS STANDING BY THE NILE, WHEN OUT OF THE RIVER THERE CAME UP SEVEN *COWS*, SLEEK AND FAT, AND THEY GRAZED AMONG THE REEDS. AFTER THEM, SEVEN OTHER COWS, UGLY AND GAUNT, CAME UP OUT OF THE NILE AND STOOD BESIDE THOSE ON THE RIVERBANK. AND THE COWS THAT WERE UGLY AND GAUNT ATE UP THE SEVEN SLEEK, FAT COWS. THEN PHARAOH WOKE UP."

GENESIS 41:1–4

HIDDEN LETTERS

ON THE NEXT PAGE, COLOR IN THE AREAS THAT
CONTAIN A SQUARE TO REVEAL THE HIDDEN
LETTERS. THEN USE THE LETTERS TO COMPLETE
THE VERSE BELOW.

"THE __ __ __ WILL FEED WITH THE
    BEAR,
      THEIR YOUNG WILL LIE DOWN
        TOGETHER,
      AND THE LION WILL EAT STRAW
        LIKE THE OX."

ISAIAH 11:7

___ ___ ___

FiNiSH the PiCTURE

USING THE GRID, DRAW THE PICTURE BELOW ON THE FOLLOWING PAGE.

COOKIES GO GOOD WITH THIS!

COLOR *the* PICTURE

"'YOU ARE A LION'S CUB, O JUDAH;
 YOU RETURN FROM THE PREY, MY SON.
LIKE A *LION* HE CROUCHES AND LIES
   DOWN,
   LIKE A LIONESS—WHO DARES TO
ROUSE HIM?'"

GENESIS 49:9

MiSSiNG PieCeS

DOES THE PICTURE ON THE NEXT PAGE LOOK A LITTLE UNFINISHED TO YOU? A LOT OF THINGS ARE LEFT OUT, BUT YOU CAN FINISH IT BY FILLING IN AS MANY MISSING PIECES AS YOU CAN FIND. LOOK CAREFULLY!

"SAMSON WENT DOWN TO TIMNAH TOGETHER WITH HIS FATHER AND MOTHER. AS THEY APPROACHED THE VINEYARDS OF TIMNAH, SUDDENLY A YOUNG *LION* CAME ROARING TOWARD HIM. THE SPIRIT OF THE LORD CAME UPON HIM IN POWER SO THAT HE TORE THE LION APART WITH HIS BARE HANDS AS HE MIGHT HAVE TORN A YOUNG GOAT. BUT HE TOLD NEITHER HIS FATHER NOR HIS MOTHER WHAT HE HAD DONE."

JUDGES 14:5-6

PiCTURE PiECES

PUT THE PICTURE PIECES IN THE RIGHT ORDER.
DRAW WHAT IS IN EACH NUMBERED BOX
BELOW INTO EACH BOX OF THE SAME NUMBER
ON THE FOLLOWING PAGE.

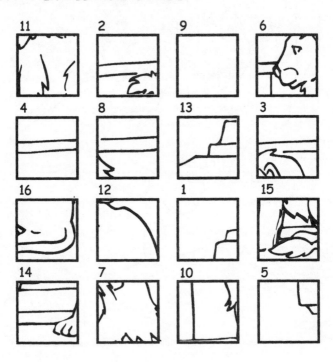

1	2	3	4
5	6	7	8
9	10	11	12
13	14	15	16

"THE THRONE HAD SIX STEPS, AND ITS BACK HAD A ROUNDED TOP. ON BOTH SIDES OF THE SEAT WERE ARMRESTS, WITH A *LION* STANDING BESIDE EACH OF THEM."

1 KINGS 10:19

WHAT'S DIFFERENT?

LOOK CAREFULLY AT THE PICTURE BELOW AND THE ONE ON THE NEXT PAGE. THEY LOOK THE SAME AT FIRST GLANCE, BUT. . .ARE THEY? CIRCLE ANY DIFFERENCES YOU FIND.

"'HE PROWLED AMONG THE *LIONS*, FOR HE WAS NOW A STRONG LION. HE LEARNED TO TEAR THE PREY AND HE DEVOURED MEN.'"

EZEKIEL 19:6

HIDDEN LETTERS

ON THE NEXT PAGE, COLOR IN THE AREAS THAT
CONTAIN A SQUARE TO REVEAL THE HIDDEN
LETTERS. THEN USE THE LETTERS TO COMPLETE
THE VERSE BELOW.

"BE SELF-CONTROLLED AND ALERT.
YOUR ENEMY THE DEVIL PROWLS
AROUND LIKE A ROARING __ __ __ __
LOOKING FOR SOMEONE TO DEVOUR."

1 PETER 5:8

___ ___ ___ ___ ___

COLOR THE PICTURE

"'I AM THE GOOD SHEPHERD. THE GOOD SHEPHERD LAYS DOWN HIS LIFE FOR THE SHEEP. THE HIRED HAND IS NOT THE SHEPHERD WHO OWNS THE SHEEP. SO WHEN HE SEES THE *WOLF* COMING, HE ABANDONS THE SHEEP AND RUNS AWAY. THEN THE WOLF ATTACKS THE FLOCK AND SCATTERS IT.'"

JOHN 10:11–12

FiNiSH *the* PiCTURE

ON THE FOLLOWING PAGE, USE THE GRID TO
COMPLETE THE PICTURE BY DUPLICATING THE
FINISHED HALF ONTO THE UNFINISHED AREA.

"'WATCH OUT FOR FALSE PROPHETS.
THEY COME TO YOU IN SHEEP'S
CLOTHING, BUT INWARDLY THEY ARE
FEROCIOUS *WOLVES*. BY THEIR FRUIT
YOU WILL RECOGNIZE THEM. DO
PEOPLE PICK GRAPES FROM THORN-
BUSHES, OR FIGS FROM THISTLES?
LIKEWISE EVERY GOOD TREE BEARS
GOOD FRUIT, BUT A BAD TREE BEARS
BAD FRUIT.'"

MATTHEW 7:15–17

MiSSiNG PieCeS

DOES THE PICTURE ON THE NEXT PAGE LOOK A LITTLE UNFINISHED TO YOU? A LOT OF THINGS ARE LEFT OUT, BUT YOU CAN FINISH IT BY FILLING IN AS MANY MISSING PIECES AS YOU CAN FIND. LOOK CAREFULLY!

"KEEP WATCH OVER YOURSELVES AND ALL THE FLOCK OF WHICH THE HOLY SPIRIT HAS MADE YOU OVERSEERS. BE SHEPHERDS OF THE CHURCH OF GOD, WHICH HE BOUGHT WITH HIS OWN BLOOD. I KNOW THAT AFTER I LEAVE, SAVAGE *WOLVES* WILL COME IN AMONG YOU AND WILL NOT SPARE THE FLOCK."

ACTS 20:28–29

PiCTURE PiECES

PUT THE PICTURE PIECES IN THE RIGHT ORDER.
DRAW WHAT IS IN EACH NUMBERED BOX
BELOW INTO EACH BOX OF THE SAME NUMBER
ON THE FOLLOWING PAGE.

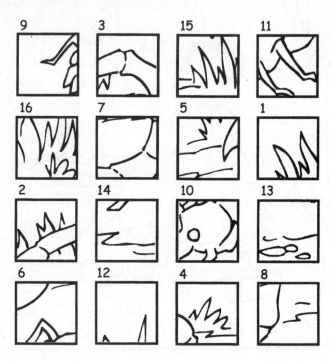

1	2	3	4
5	6	7	8
9	10	11	12
13	14	15	16

"AND THE AGONY THEY SUFFERED WAS LIKE THAT OF THE STING OF A *SCORPION* WHEN IT STRIKES A MAN."

REVELATION 9:5

COLOR THE PICTURE

"*ANTS* ARE CREATURES OF LITTLE STRENGTH, YET THEY STORE UP THEIR FOOD IN THE SUMMER."

PROVERBS 30:25

WHAT'S DIFFERENT?

LOOK CAREFULLY AT THE PICTURE BELOW AND THE ONE ON THE NEXT PAGE. THEY LOOK THE SAME AT FIRST GLANCE, BUT. . .ARE THEY? CIRCLE ANY DIFFERENCES YOU FIND.

"GO TO THE *ANT*, YOU SLUGGARD;
   CONSIDER ITS WAYS AND BE WISE!"

PROVERBS 6:6

COLOR THE PICTURE

"IT IS GOD WHO ARMS ME WITH
    STRENGTH
    AND MAKES MY WAY PERFECT.
HE MAKES MY FEET LIKE THE FEET OF
    A *DEER*;
HE ENABLES ME TO STAND ON THE
    HEIGHTS."

PSALM 18:32–33

FiNiSH the PiCTURE

USING THE GRID, DRAW THE PICTURE BELOW ON THE FOLLOWING PAGE.

DOE, A DEER

HIDDEN LETTERS

ON THE NEXT PAGE, COLOR IN THE AREAS THAT CONTAIN A SQUARE TO REVEAL THE HIDDEN LETTERS. THEN USE THE LETTERS TO COMPLETE THE VERSE BELOW.

"'BUT AMONG THE ISRAELITES NOT A ___ ___ ___ WILL BARK AT ANY MAN OR ANIMAL.' THEN YOU WILL KNOW THAT THE LORD MAKES A DISTINCTION BETWEEN EGYPT AND ISRAEL."

EXODUS 11:7

— — —

PiCTURE PiECES

PUT THE PICTURE PIECES IN THE RIGHT ORDER. DRAW WHAT IS IN EACH NUMBERED BOX BELOW INTO EACH BOX OF THE SAME NUMBER ON THE FOLLOWING PAGE.

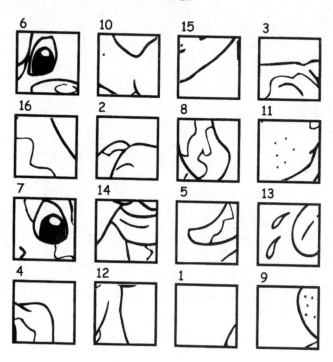

1	2	3	4
5	6	7	8
9	10	11	12
13	14	15	16

"SO GIDEON TOOK THE MEN DOWN TO THE WATER. THERE THE LORD TOLD HIM, 'SEPARATE THOSE WHO LAP THE WATER WITH THEIR TONGUES LIKE A *DOG* FROM THOSE WHO KNEEL DOWN TO DRINK.'"

JUDGES 7:5

FiNiSH *the* PiCTURE

ON THE FOLLOWING PAGE, USE THE GRID TO
COMPLETE THE PICTURE BY DUPLICATING THE
FINISHED HALF ONTO THE UNFINISHED AREA.

"'I TELL YOU THE TRUTH,' JESUS
ANSWERED, 'THIS VERY NIGHT, BEFORE
THE *ROOSTER* CROWS, YOU WILL
DISOWN ME THREE TIMES.'"

MATTHEW 26:34

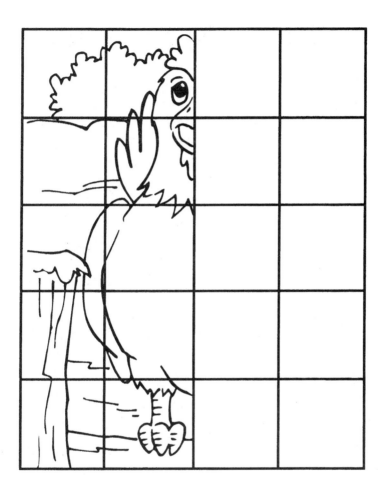

MISSING PIECES

DOES THE PICTURE ON THE NEXT PAGE LOOK A LITTLE UNFINISHED TO YOU? A LOT OF THINGS ARE LEFT OUT, BUT YOU CAN FINISH IT BY FILLING IN AS MANY MISSING PIECES AS YOU CAN FIND. LOOK CAREFULLY!

"ONE OF THE HIGH PRIEST'S SERVANTS, A RELATIVE OF THE MAN WHOSE EAR PETER HAD CUT OFF, CHALLENGED HIM, 'DIDN'T I SEE YOU WITH HIM IN THE OLIVE GROVE?' AGAIN PETER DENIED IT, AND AT THAT MOMENT A *ROOSTER* BEGAN TO CROW."

JOHN 18:26-27

COLOR *THE* PICTURE

"A *LIZARD* CAN BE CAUGHT WITH THE HAND,
    YET IT IS FOUND IN KINGS' PALACES."

PROVERBS 30:28

WHAT'S DIFFERENT?

LOOK CAREFULLY AT THE PICTURE BELOW AND THE ONE ON THE NEXT PAGE. THEY LOOK THE SAME AT FIRST GLANCE, BUT. . .ARE THEY? CIRCLE ANY DIFFERENCES YOU FIND.

"'THE GECKO, THE MONITOR LIZARD, THE WALL LIZARD, THE SKINK AND THE *CHAMELEON.*'"

LEVITICUS 11:30

HIDDEN LETTERS

ON THE NEXT PAGE, COLOR IN THE AREAS THAT CONTAIN A SQUARE TO REVEAL THE HIDDEN LETTERS. THEN USE THE LETTERS TO COMPLETE THE VERSE BELOW.

"THE LORD SAID, 'THROW IT ON THE GROUND.' MOSES THREW IT ON THE GROUND AND IT BECAME A __ __ __ __ __, AND HE RAN FROM IT. THEN THE LORD SAID TO HIM, 'REACH OUT YOUR HAND AND TAKE IT BY THE TAIL.' SO MOSES REACHED OUT AND TOOK HOLD OF THE SNAKE AND IT TURNED BACK INTO A STAFF IN HIS HAND."

EXODUS 4:3–4

__ __ __ __ __

FiNiSH *the* PiCTURE

ON THE FOLLOWING PAGE, USE THE GRID TO
COMPLETE THE PICTURE BY DUPLICATING THE
FINISHED HALF ONTO THE UNFINISHED AREA.

"FOR HE WILL COMMAND HIS ANGELS
    CONCERNING YOU
  TO GUARD YOU IN ALL YOUR WAYS;
THEY WILL LIFT YOU UP IN THEIR
  HANDS,
SO THAT YOU WILL NOT STRIKE YOUR
  FOOT AGAINST A STONE.
YOU WILL TREAD UPON THE LION AND
  THE *COBRA*;
YOU WILL TRAMPLE THE GREAT LION
  AND THE SERPENT."

PSALM 91:11–13

PICTURE PIECES

PUT THE PICTURE PIECES IN THE RIGHT ORDER.
DRAW WHAT IS IN EACH NUMBERED BOX
BELOW INTO EACH BOX OF THE SAME NUMBER
ON THE FOLLOWING PAGE.

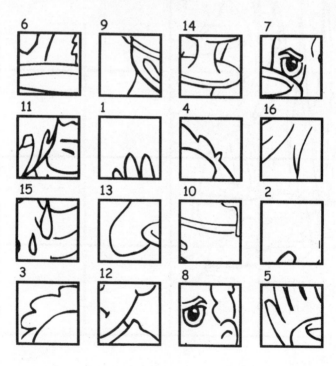

1	2	3	4
5	6	7	8
9	10	11	12
13	14	15	16

"DO NOT GAZE AT WINE WHEN IT
   IS RED,
   WHEN IT SPARKLES IN THE CUP,
   WHEN IT GOES DOWN SMOOTHLY!
IN THE END IT BITES LIKE A *SNAKE*
   AND POISONS LIKE A VIPER."

PROVERBS 23:31–32

FiNiSH *the* PiCTURE

USING THE GRID, DRAW THE PICTURE BELOW
ON THE FOLLOWING PAGE.

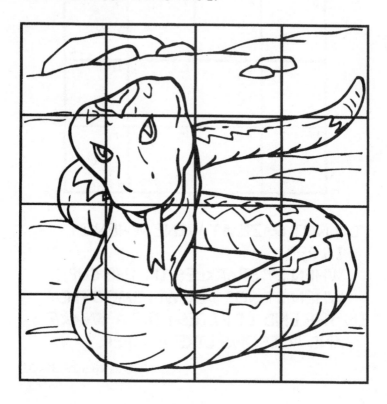

FEET...GET READY TO RUN!

COLOR THE PICTURE

"THEN ANOTHER SIGN APPEARED IN HEAVEN: AN ENORMOUS *RED DRAGON* WITH SEVEN HEADS AND TEN HORNS AND SEVEN CROWNS ON HIS HEADS."

REVELATION 12:3

Missing Pieces

DOES THE PICTURE ON THE NEXT PAGE LOOK A LITTLE UNFINISHED TO YOU? A LOT OF THINGS ARE LEFT OUT, BUT YOU CAN FINISH IT BY FILLING IN AS MANY MISSING PIECES AS YOU CAN FIND. LOOK CAREFULLY!

"AND THERE WAS WAR IN HEAVEN. MICHAEL AND HIS ANGELS FOUGHT AGAINST THE *DRAGON*, AND THE DRAGON AND HIS ANGELS FOUGHT BACK. BUT HE WAS NOT STRONG ENOUGH, AND THEY LOST THEIR PLACE IN HEAVEN."

REVELATION 12:7–8

WHAT'S DIFFERENT?

LOOK CAREFULLY AT THE PICTURE BELOW AND THE ONE ON THE NEXT PAGE. THEY LOOK THE SAME AT FIRST GLANCE, BUT. . .ARE THEY? CIRCLE ANY DIFFERENCES YOU FIND.

"THEN THE LORD SAID TO MOSES, 'TELL AARON, "STRETCH OUT YOUR HAND WITH YOUR STAFF OVER THE STREAMS AND CANALS AND PONDS, AND MAKE *FROGS* COME UP ON THE LAND OF EGYPT."'"

EXODUS 8:5

FiNiSH *the* PiCTURE

ON THE FOLLOWING PAGE, USE THE GRID TO
COMPLETE THE PICTURE BY DUPLICATING THE
FINISHED HALF ONTO THE UNFINISHED AREA.

"THE *OWL* WILL NEST THERE AND LAY
     EGGS,
   SHE WILL HATCH THEM, AND CARE
     FOR HER YOUNG UNDER THE
     SHADOW OF HER WINGS;
THERE ALSO THE FALCONS WILL GATHER,
   EACH WITH ITS MATE."

ISAIAH 34:15

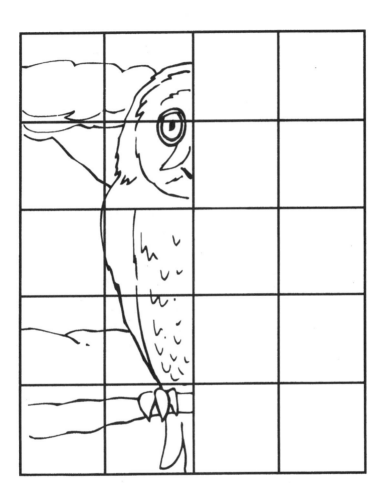

HIDDEN LETTERS

ON THE NEXT PAGE, COLOR IN THE AREAS THAT CONTAIN A SQUARE TO REVEAL THE HIDDEN LETTERS. THEN USE THE LETTERS TO COMPLETE THE VERSE BELOW.

"BECAUSE OF MY LOUD GROANING
   I AM REDUCED TO SKIN AND BONES.
I AM LIKE A DESERT __ __ __,
   LIKE AN OWL AMONG THE RUINS.
I LIE AWAKE; I HAVE BECOME
   LIKE A BIRD ALONE ON A ROOF.
ALL DAY LONG MY ENEMIES TAUNT ME;
   THOSE WHO RAIL AGAINST ME USE
      MY NAME AS A CURSE."

PSALM 102:5–8

___ _ ___

105

COLOR THE PICTURE

"'SO DESERT CREATURES AND *HYENAS*
WILL LIVE THERE,
AND THERE THE OWL WILL DWELL.
IT WILL NEVER AGAIN BE INHABITED
OR LIVED IN FROM GENERATION TO
GENERATION.'"

JEREMIAH 50:39

PICTURE PIECES

PUT THE PICTURE PIECES IN THE RIGHT ORDER.
DRAW WHAT IS IN EACH NUMBERED BOX
BELOW INTO EACH BOX OF THE SAME NUMBER
ON THE FOLLOWING PAGE.

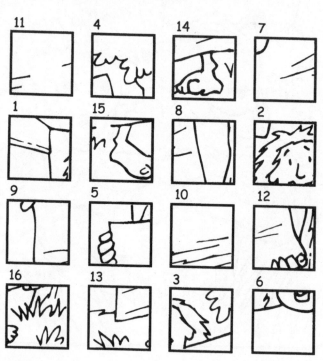

1	2	3	4
5	6	7	8
9	10	11	12
13	14	15	16

"BECAUSE OF THIS I WILL WEEP AND WAIL;
I WILL GO ABOUT BAREFOOT AND NAKED.
I WILL HOWL LIKE A *JACKAL*
AND MOAN LIKE AN OWL."

MICAH 1:8

Missing Pieces

DOES THE PICTURE ON THE NEXT PAGE LOOK A LITTLE UNFINISHED TO YOU? A LOT OF THINGS ARE LEFT OUT, BUT YOU CAN FINISH IT BY FILLING IN AS MANY MISSING PIECES AS YOU CAN FIND. LOOK CAREFULLY!

"AND THE LORD SAID TO MOSES, 'STRETCH OUT YOUR HAND OVER EGYPT SO THAT *LOCUSTS* WILL SWARM OVER THE LAND AND DEVOUR EVERYTHING GROWING IN THE FIELDS, EVERYTHING LEFT BY THE HAIL.'"

EXODUS 10:12

WHAT'S DIFFERENT?

LOOK CAREFULLY AT THE PICTURE BELOW AND THE ONE ON THE NEXT PAGE. THEY LOOK THE SAME AT FIRST GLANCE, BUT. . .ARE THEY? CIRCLE ANY DIFFERENCES YOU FIND.

"FOR I AM POOR AND NEEDY, AND MY HEART IS WOUNDED WITHIN ME. I FADE AWAY LIKE AN EVENING SHADOW; I AM SHAKEN OFF LIKE A *LOCUST.*"

PSALM 109:22–23

FiNiSH the PiCTURE

USING THE GRID, DRAW THE PICTURE BELOW
ON THE FOLLOWING PAGE.

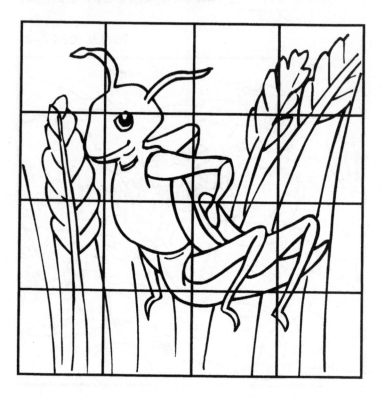

A BIG APPETITE FOR A LITTLE GUY

FiNiSH the PiCTURE

ON THE FOLLOWING PAGE, USE THE GRID TO COMPLETE THE PICTURE BY DUPLICATING THE FINISHED HALF ONTO THE UNFINISHED AREA.

"OF THESE YOU MAY EAT ANY KIND OF LOCUST, KATYDID, *CRICKET* OR *GRASSHOPPER*. BUT ALL OTHER WINGED CREATURES THAT HAVE FOUR LEGS YOU ARE TO DETEST."

LEVITICUS 11:22–23

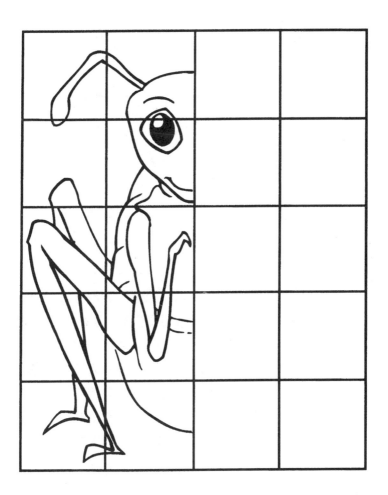

117

COLOR the PICTURE

"ABRAHAM LOOKED UP AND THERE IN A THICKET HE SAW A *RAM* CAUGHT BY ITS HORNS. HE WENT OVER AND TOOK THE RAM AND SACRIFICED IT AS A BURNT OFFERING INSTEAD OF HIS SON. SO ABRAHAM CALLED THAT PLACE THE LORD WILL PROVIDE. AND TO THIS DAY IT IS SAID, 'ON THE MOUNTAIN OF THE LORD IT WILL BE PROVIDED.'"

GENESIS 22:13–14

PiCTURE PiECES

PUT THE PICTURE PIECES IN THE RIGHT ORDER. DRAW WHAT IS IN EACH NUMBERED BOX BELOW INTO EACH BOX OF THE SAME NUMBER ON THE FOLLOWING PAGE.

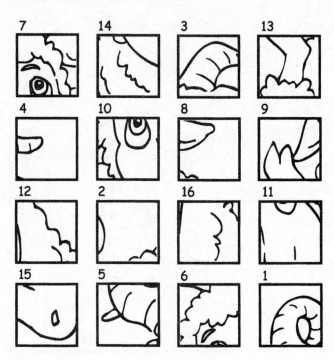

1	2	3	4
5	6	7	8
9	10	11	12
13	14	15	16

"I LOOKED UP, AND THERE BEFORE ME WAS A *RAM* WITH TWO HORNS, STANDING BESIDE THE CANAL, AND THE HORNS WERE LONG. ONE OF THE HORNS WAS LONGER THAN THE OTHER BUT GREW UP LATER."

DANIEL 8:3

COLOR the PICTURE

"AS I WATCHED, I HEARD AN *EAGLE* THAT WAS FLYING IN MIDAIR CALL OUT IN A LOUD VOICE: 'WOE! WOE! WOE TO THE INHABITANTS OF THE EARTH, BECAUSE OF THE TRUMPET BLASTS ABOUT TO BE SOUNDED BY THE OTHER THREE ANGELS!'"

REVELATION 8:13

HIDDEN LETTERS

ON THE NEXT PAGE, COLOR IN THE AREAS THAT CONTAIN A SQUARE TO REVEAL THE HIDDEN LETTERS. THEN USE THE LETTERS TO COMPLETE THE VERSE BELOW.

"CAST BUT A GLANCE AT RICHES, AND
     THEY ARE GONE,
   FOR THEY WILL SURELY SPROUT
     WINGS
   AND FLY OFF TO THE SKY LIKE AN
   __ __ __ __ __."

PROVERBS 23:5

_ _ _ _ _ _

125

FiNiSH *the* PiCTURE

ON THE FOLLOWING PAGE, USE THE GRID TO
COMPLETE THE PICTURE BY DUPLICATING THE
FINISHED HALF ONTO THE UNFINISHED AREA.

"IN A DESERT LAND HE FOUND HIM,
   IN A BARREN AND HOWLING
      WASTE.
HE SHIELDED HIM AND CARED FOR HIM;
   HE GUARDED HIM AS THE APPLE OF
      HIS EYE,
LIKE AN *EAGLE* THAT STIRS UP ITS NEST
   AND HOVERS OVER ITS YOUNG,
THAT SPREADS ITS WINGS TO CATCH
      THEM
     AND CARRIES THEM ON ITS
      PINIONS."

DEUTERONOMY 32:10–11

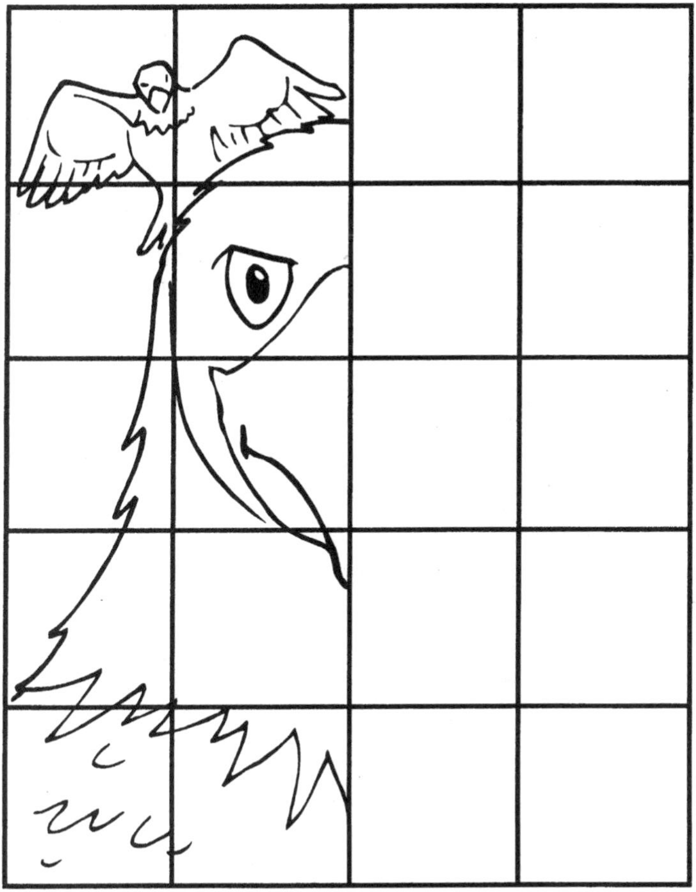

MISSING PIECES

DOES THE PICTURE ON THE NEXT PAGE LOOK A LITTLE UNFINISHED TO YOU? A LOT OF THINGS ARE LEFT OUT, BUT YOU CAN FINISH IT BY FILLING IN AS MANY MISSING PIECES AS YOU CAN FIND. LOOK CAREFULLY!

"YOUR SONS HAVE FAINTED;
    THEY LIE AT THE HEAD OF EVERY
        STREET,
    LIKE *ANTELOPE* CAUGHT IN A NET.
THEY ARE FILLED WITH THE WRATH
        OF THE LORD
    AND THE REBUKE OF YOUR GOD."

ISAIAH 51:20

FiNiSH the PiCTURE

USING THE GRID, DRAW THE PICTURE BELOW ON THE FOLLOWING PAGE.

CUTE AS A BUNNY!

COLOR the PICTURE

"HUSHAI REPLIED TO ABSALOM, 'THE ADVICE AHITHOPHEL HAS GIVEN IS NOT GOOD THIS TIME. YOU KNOW YOUR FATHER AND HIS MEN; THEY ARE FIGHTERS, AND AS FIERCE AS A WILD *BEAR* ROBBED OF HER CUBS.'"

2 SAMUEL 17:7-8

WHAT'S DIFFERENT?

LOOK CAREFULLY AT THE PICTURE BELOW AND THE ONE ON THE NEXT PAGE. THEY LOOK THE SAME AT FIRST GLANCE, BUT. . .ARE THEY? CIRCLE ANY DIFFERENCES YOU FIND.

"BUT DAVID SAID TO SAUL, 'YOUR SERVANT HAS BEEN KEEPING HIS FATHER'S SHEEP. WHEN A LION OR A *BEAR* CAME AND CARRIED OFF A SHEEP FROM THE FLOCK, I WENT AFTER IT, STRUCK IT AND RESCUED THE SHEEP FROM ITS MOUTH.'"

1 SAMUEL 17:34–35

PiCTURE PiECES

PUT THE PICTURE PIECES IN THE RIGHT ORDER. DRAW WHAT IS IN EACH NUMBERED BOX BELOW INTO EACH BOX OF THE SAME NUMBER ON THE FOLLOWING PAGE.

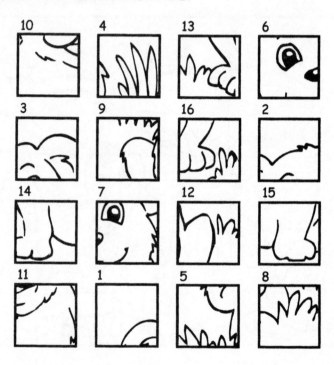

1	2	3	4
5	6	7	8
9	10	11	12
13	14	15	16

"'CAN YOU BRING FORTH THE CONSTELLATIONS IN THEIR SEASONS OR LEAD OUT THE *BEAR* WITH ITS CUBS?'"

JOB 38:32

HIDDEN LETTERS

ON THE NEXT PAGE, COLOR IN THE AREAS THAT
CONTAIN A SQUARE TO REVEAL THE HIDDEN
LETTERS. THEN USE THE LETTERS TO COMPLETE
THE VERSE BELOW.

"BETTER TO MEET A __ __ __ __
ROBBED OF HER CUBS
THAN A FOOL IN HIS FOLLY."

PROVERBS 17:12

FiNiSH the PiCTURE

USING THE GRID, DRAW THE PICTURE BELOW
ON THE FOLLOWING PAGE.

IS "TEDDY" HIS NAME?

COLOR THE PICTURE

"IN THOSE DAYS I SAW MEN IN JUDAH TREADING WINEPRESSES ON THE SABBATH AND BRINGING IN GRAIN AND LOADING IT ON DONKEYS, TOGETHER WITH WINE, GRAPES, FIGS AND ALL OTHER KINDS OF LOADS. AND THEY WERE BRINGING ALL THIS INTO JERUSALEM ON THE SABBATH. THEREFORE I WARNED THEM AGAINST SELLING FOOD ON THAT DAY. MEN FROM TYRE WHO LIVED IN JERUSALEM WERE BRINGING IN *FISH* AND ALL KINDS OF MERCHANDISE AND SELLING THEM IN JERUSALEM ON THE SABBATH TO THE PEOPLE OF JUDAH."

NEHEMIAH 13:15–16

Missing Pieces

DOES THE PICTURE ON THE NEXT PAGE LOOK A LITTLE UNFINISHED TO YOU? A LOT OF THINGS ARE LEFT OUT, BUT YOU CAN FINISH IT BY FILLING IN AS MANY MISSING PIECES AS YOU CAN FIND. LOOK CAREFULLY!

"THEN GOD SAID, 'LET US MAKE MAN IN OUR IMAGE, IN OUR LIKENESS, AND LET THEM RULE OVER THE *FISH* OF THE SEA AND THE BIRDS OF THE AIR, OVER THE LIVESTOCK, OVER ALL THE EARTH, AND OVER ALL THE CREATURES THAT MOVE ALONG THE GROUND.'"

GENESIS 1:26

145

WHAT'S DIFFERENT?

LOOK CAREFULLY AT THE PICTURE BELOW AND THE ONE ON THE NEXT PAGE. THEY LOOK THE SAME AT FIRST GLANCE, BUT. . .ARE THEY? CIRCLE ANY DIFFERENCES YOU FIND.

"'ONCE AGAIN, THE KINGDOM OF HEAVEN IS LIKE A NET THAT WAS LET DOWN INTO THE LAKE AND CAUGHT ALL KINDS OF *FISH*.'"

MATTHEW 13:47

FiNiSH *the* PiCTURE

ON THE FOLLOWING PAGE, USE THE GRID TO
COMPLETE THE PICTURE BY DUPLICATING THE
FINISHED HALF ONTO THE UNFINISHED AREA.

"TAKING THE FIVE LOAVES AND THE
TWO *FISH* AND LOOKING UP TO
HEAVEN, HE GAVE THANKS AND BROKE
THEM. THEN HE GAVE THEM TO THE
DISCIPLES TO SET BEFORE THE PEOPLE.
THEY ALL ATE AND WERE SATISFIED,
AND THE DISCIPLES PICKED UP TWELVE
BASKETFULS OF BROKEN PIECES THAT
WERE LEFT OVER."

LUKE 9:16–17

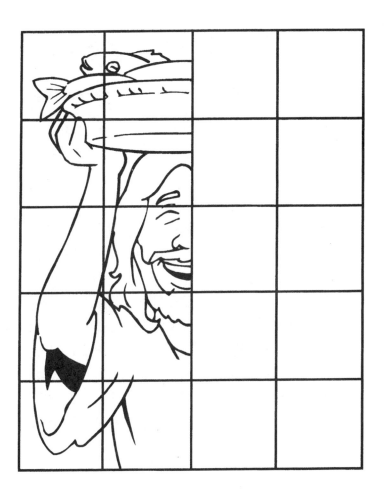

149

HIDDEN LETTERS

ON THE NEXT PAGE, COLOR IN THE AREAS THAT CONTAIN A SQUARE TO REVEAL THE HIDDEN LETTERS. THEN USE THE LETTERS TO COMPLETE THE VERSE BELOW.

"WHEN YOU SOW, YOU DO NOT PLANT THE BODY THAT WILL BE, BUT JUST A SEED, PERHAPS OF WHEAT OR OF SOMETHING ELSE. BUT GOD GIVES IT A BODY AS HE HAS DETERMINED, AND TO EACH KIND OF SEED HE GIVES ITS OWN BODY. ALL FLESH IS NOT THE SAME: MEN HAVE ONE KIND OF FLESH, ANIMALS HAVE ANOTHER, BIRDS ANOTHER AND __ __ __ __ ANOTHER."

1 CORINTHIANS 15:37–39

MISSING PIECES

DOES THE PICTURE ON THE NEXT PAGE LOOK A LITTLE UNFINISHED TO YOU? A LOT OF THINGS ARE LEFT OUT, BUT YOU CAN FINISH IT BY FILLING IN AS MANY MISSING PIECES AS YOU CAN FIND. LOOK CAREFULLY!

"'A WICKED AND ADULTEROUS GENERATION ASKS FOR A MIRACULOUS SIGN! BUT NONE WILL BE GIVEN IT EXCEPT THE SIGN OF THE PROPHET JONAH. FOR AS JONAH WAS THREE DAYS AND THREE NIGHTS IN THE BELLY OF A HUGE *FISH*, SO THE SON OF MAN WILL BE THREE DAYS AND THREE NIGHTS IN THE HEART OF THE EARTH.'"

MATTHEW 12:39–40

FiNiSH *the* PiCTURE

ON THE FOLLOWING PAGE, USE THE GRID TO COMPLETE THE PICTURE BY DUPLICATING THE FINISHED HALF ONTO THE UNFINISHED AREA.

"BUT THE LORD PROVIDED A GREAT *FISH* TO SWALLOW JONAH, AND JONAH WAS INSIDE THE FISH THREE DAYS AND THREE NIGHTS."

JONAH 1:17

154

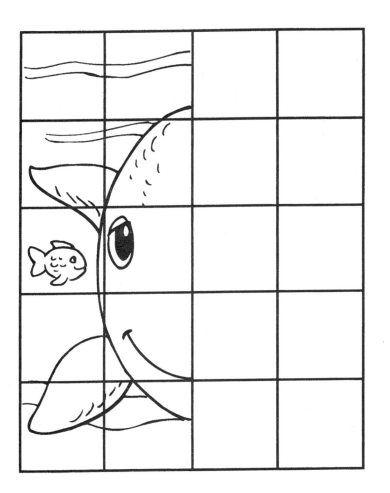

COLOR THE PICTURE

"'LOOK AT THE *BEHEMOTH*,
     WHICH I MADE ALONG WITH YOU
     AND WHICH FEEDS ON GRASS LIKE
     AN OX.
WHAT STRENGTH HE HAS IN HIS
     LOINS,
WHAT POWER IN THE MUSCLES OF HIS
     BELLY!
HIS TAIL SWAYS LIKE A CEDAR;
     THE SINEWS OF HIS THIGHS ARE
     CLOSE-KNIT.
HIS BONES ARE TUBES OF BRONZE,
     HIS LIMBS LIKE RODS OF IRON.
HE RANKS FIRST AMONG THE WORKS
     OF GOD,
YET HIS MAKER CAN APPROACH HIM
     WITH HIS SWORD.'"

JOB 40:15–19

FiNiSH *the* PiCTURE

USING THE GRID, DRAW THE PICTURE BELOW ON THE FOLLOWING PAGE.

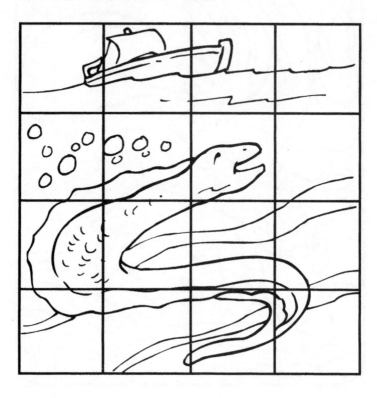

158

LEVIATHAN...OR SOMETHING ELSE?

PiCTURE PiECES

PUT THE PICTURE PIECES IN THE RIGHT ORDER.
DRAW WHAT IS IN EACH NUMBERED BOX
BELOW INTO EACH BOX OF THE SAME NUMBER
ON THE FOLLOWING PAGE.

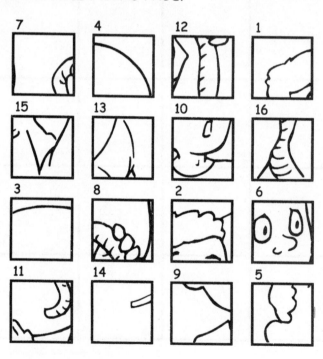

1	2	3	4
5	6	7	8
9	10	11	12
13	14	15	16

"'CAN YOU PULL IN THE *LEVIATHAN*
WITH A FISHHOOK
OR TIE DOWN HIS TONGUE WITH A
ROPE?'"

JOB 41:1

COLOR the PICTURE

"IN THE BEGINNING GOD CREATED THE HEAVENS AND THE EARTH. NOW THE EARTH WAS FORMLESS AND EMPTY, DARKNESS WAS OVER THE SURFACE OF THE DEEP, AND THE SPIRIT OF GOD WAS HOVERING OVER THE WATERS."

GENESIS 1:1–2

163

HIDDEN LETTERS

ON THE NEXT PAGE, COLOR IN THE AREAS THAT
CONTAIN A SQUARE TO REVEAL THE HIDDEN
LETTERS. THEN USE THE LETTERS TO COMPLETE
THE VERSE BELOW.

"SO GOD CREATED THE GREAT
CREATURES OF THE SEA AND EVERY
LIVING AND MOVING THING WITH
WHICH THE WATER TEEMS,
ACCORDING TO THEIR KINDS, AND
EVERY WINGED __ __ __ __
ACCORDING TO ITS KIND. AND GOD
SAW THAT IT WAS GOOD. GOD
BLESSED THEM AND SAID, 'BE
FRUITFUL AND INCREASE IN
NUMBER AND FILL THE WATER IN THE
SEAS, AND LET THE BIRDS INCREASE
ON THE EARTH.'"

GENESIS 1:21-22

___ ___ ___ ___

MiSSiNG PieCeS

DOES THE PICTURE ON THE NEXT PAGE LOOK A LITTLE UNFINISHED TO YOU? A LOT OF THINGS ARE LEFT OUT, BUT YOU CAN FINISH IT BY FILLING IN AS MANY MISSING PIECES AS YOU CAN FIND. LOOK CAREFULLY!

"AND GOD SAID, 'LET THE LAND PRODUCE LIVING CREATURES ACCORDING TO THEIR KINDS: LIVESTOCK, CREATURES THAT MOVE ALONG THE GROUND, AND WILD ANIMALS, EACH ACCORDING TO ITS KIND.' AND IT WAS SO. GOD MADE THE WILD ANIMALS ACCORDING TO THEIR KINDS, THE LIVESTOCK ACCORDING TO THEIR KINDS, AND ALL THE CREATURES THAT MOVE ALONG THE GROUND ACCORDING TO THEIR KINDS. AND GOD SAW THAT IT WAS GOOD."

GENESIS 1:24–25

FiNiSH *the* PiCTURE

USING THE GRID, DRAW THE PICTURE BELOW
ON THE FOLLOWING PAGE.

A BIG ONE!

FiNiSH *the* PiCTURE

ON THE FOLLOWING PAGE, USE THE GRID TO
COMPLETE THE PICTURE BY DUPLICATING THE
FINISHED HALF ONTO THE UNFINISHED AREA.

"THEN GOD SAID, 'LET US MAKE MAN IN
OUR IMAGE, IN OUR LIKENESS, AND
LET THEM RULE OVER THE FISH OF THE
SEA AND THE BIRDS OF THE AIR, OVER
THE LIVESTOCK, OVER ALL THE EARTH,
AND OVER ALL THE CREATURES THAT
MOVE ALONG THE GROUND.'. . .GOD
BLESSED THEM AND SAID TO THEM, 'BE
FRUITFUL AND INCREASE IN NUMBER;
FILL THE EARTH AND SUBDUE IT. RULE
OVER THE FISH OF THE SEA AND THE
BIRDS OF THE AIR AND OVER EVERY
LIVING CREATURE THAT MOVES ON
THE GROUND.'"

GENESIS 1:26, 28

COLOR the PICTURE

"THEN GOD SAID, 'I GIVE YOU EVERY SEED-BEARING PLANT ON THE FACE OF THE WHOLE EARTH AND EVERY TREE THAT HAS FRUIT WITH SEED IN IT. THEY WILL BE YOURS FOR FOOD. AND TO ALL THE BEASTS OF THE EARTH AND ALL THE BIRDS OF THE AIR AND ALL THE CREATURES THAT MOVE ON THE GROUND—EVERYTHING THAT HAS THE BREATH OF LIFE IN IT—I GIVE EVERY GREEN PLANT FOR FOOD.' AND IT WAS SO. GOD SAW ALL THAT HE HAD MADE, AND IT WAS VERY GOOD. AND THERE WAS EVENING, AND THERE WAS MORNING—THE SIXTH DAY."

GENESIS 1:29–31

ABRAHAM

WHO *WAS* ABRAHAM? WHY WAS THIS MAN SO IMPORTANT?

ABRAHAM WAS CALLED RIGHTEOUS. WHY? WAS HE A GOOD PERSON? DID HE ALWAYS DO WHAT WAS RIGHT? DID HE EVER DO SOMETHING WRONG WHEN HE WAS AFRAID? DID HE ALWAYS TRUST GOD? DID HE EVER TELL A LIE? DID HE EVER ASK ANOTHER TO TELL A LIE FOR HIM? WAS ABRAHAM CONSIDERED RIGHTEOUS BY HOW HE LIVED AND ACTED, OR BECAUSE HE BELIEVED GOD AND HIS PROMISES?

IN YOUR BIBLE, READ THE STORY OF ABRAHAM YOURSELF, AND AS YOU READ THE VERSES THROUGHOUT THIS BOOK, LOOK FOR THE ANSWERS TO THESE QUESTIONS.

THEN ASK YOURSELF, *HOW DOES THIS STORY RELATE TO ME, MY LIFE, AND MY CHOICES TODAY? HOW DOES GOD VIEW ME AND WHAT I DO? WHO DO I BELIEVE: MYSELF, PEOPLE, OR GOD?*

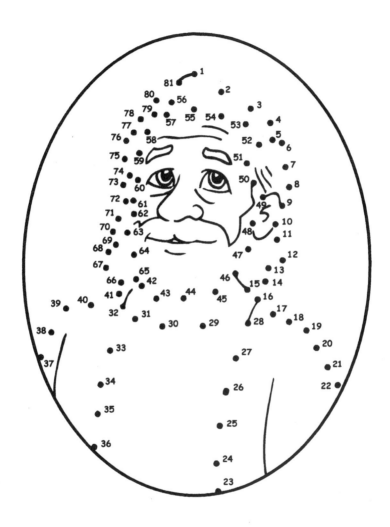

175

ABRAHAM OR ABRAM?

ABRAHAM BEGAN HIS LIFE WITH THE NAME OF *ABRAM*. AT SOME TIME IN THE FUTURE, GOD CHANGED HIS NAME. AS YOU GO THROUGH THIS STORY, YOU WILL FIND OUT WHEN AND WHY THE LORD CHANGED THE NAME OF THIS WELL-KNOWN MAN.

"TERAH TOOK HIS SON ABRAM, HIS GRANDSON LOT SON OF HARAN, AND HIS DAUGHTER-IN-LAW SARAI, THE WIFE OF HIS SON ABRAM, AND TOGETHER THEY SET OUT FROM UR OF THE CHALDEANS TO GO TO CANAAN. BUT WHEN THEY CAME TO HARAN, THEY SETTLED THERE."

GENESIS 11:31

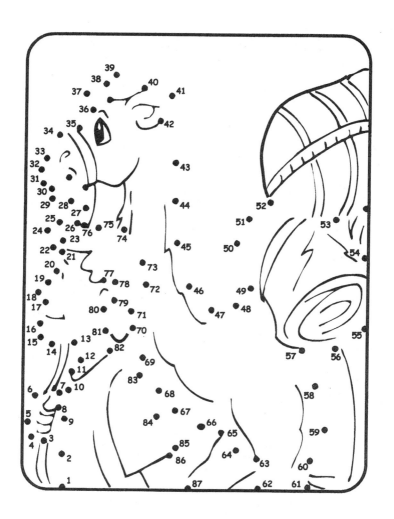

177

TIME TO MOVE OUT

HAVE YOU EVER WONDERED HOW GOD SPOKE TO ABRAM?

"THE LORD HAD SAID TO ABRAM, 'LEAVE YOUR COUNTRY, YOUR PEOPLE AND YOUR FATHER'S HOUSEHOLD AND GO TO THE LAND I WILL SHOW YOU.'"

GENESIS 12:1

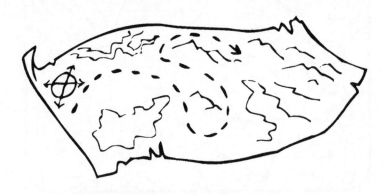

179

I WILL BLESS YOU

WHY DO YOU THINK GOD CHOSE TO MAKE ABRAM INTO A GREAT NATION?

"'I WILL MAKE YOU INTO A GREAT NATION AND I WILL BLESS YOU; I WILL MAKE YOUR NAME GREAT, AND YOU WILL BE A BLESSING.'"

GENESIS 12:2

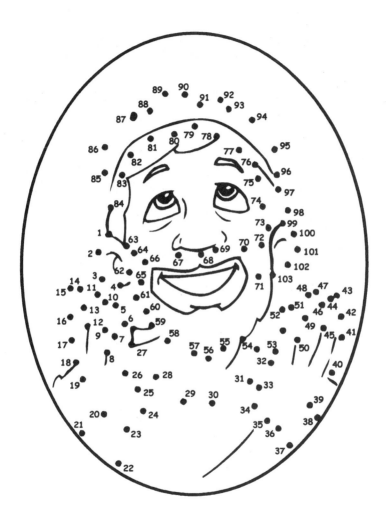

181

MORE BLESSINGS

WHY WILL ALL PEOPLE ON EARTH BE BLESSED THROUGH ABRAM?

" 'I WILL BLESS THOSE WHO BLESS YOU, AND WHOEVER CURSES YOU I WILL CURSE; AND ALL PEOPLES ON EARTH WILL BE BLESSED THROUGH YOU.' "

GENESIS 12:3

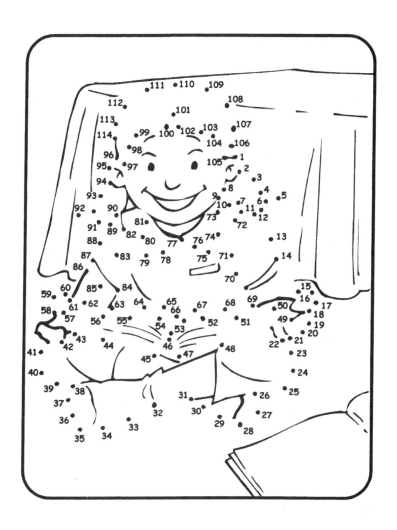

183

ON THE ROAD AGAIN

DO YOU EVER WONDER WHAT WAS GOING THROUGH ABRAM'S MIND WHEN GOD ASKED HIM TO MOVE AGAIN? HAVE YOU EVER HAD TO MOVE AGAIN WHEN YOU WERE JUST GETTING SETTLED IN? HOW DID IT MAKE *YOU* FEEL?

"SO ABRAM LEFT, AS THE LORD HAD TOLD HIM; AND LOT WENT WITH HIM. ABRAM WAS SEVENTY-FIVE YEARS OLD WHEN HE SET OUT FROM HARAN."

GENESIS 12:4

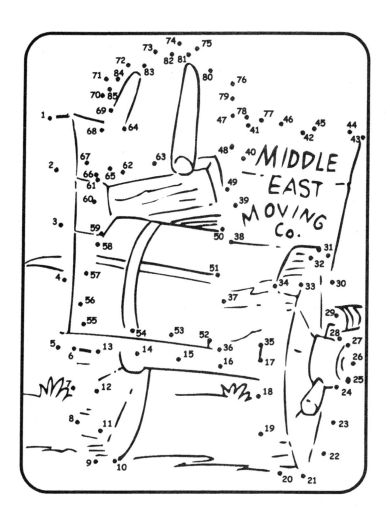

MIDDLE EAST MOVING Co.

THE LORD APPEARED

HOW DID THE LORD APPEAR TO ABRAM?

"ABRAM TRAVELED THROUGH THE LAND AS FAR AS THE SITE OF THE GREAT TREE OF MOREH AT SHECHEM. AT THAT TIME THE CANAANITES WERE IN THE LAND. THE LORD APPEARED TO ABRAM AND SAID, 'TO YOUR OFFSPRING I WILL GIVE THIS LAND.' SO HE BUILT AN ALTAR THERE TO THE LORD, WHO HAD APPEARED TO HIM."

GENESIS 12:6–7

187

THINK, THINK, THINK

TERAH TOOK HIS SON, ABRAM, HIS GRANDSON, LOT, AND ABRAM'S WIFE, SARAI TO THE LAND OF HARAN. JUST WHEN THEY WERE SETTLING IN AND STARTING TO FEEL AT HOME, GOD TOLD ABRAM TO LEAVE HIS COUNTRY AND HIS FATHER'S HOUSEHOLD. GOD DIDN'T STOP THERE! HE DIDN'T TELL ABRAM *WHERE* HE WAS GOING. WHAT DID ABRAM DO? HE DID AS GOD ASKED HIM TO DO.

WHAT WOULD *YOU* HAVE DONE IF YOU WERE ABRAM? WOULD YOU HAVE DONE WHAT GOD ASKED YOU TO DO EVEN THOUGH YOU DIDN'T KNOW WHERE YOU WERE GOING?

THINK, THINK, THINK!

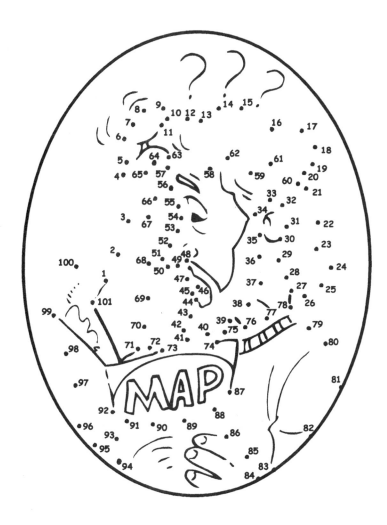

189

I'M SO HUNGRY!

WHAT DOES IT MEAN WHEN SOMEONE SAYS THERE IS A FAMINE IN THE LAND?

"NOW THERE WAS A FAMINE IN THE LAND, AND ABRAM WENT DOWN TO EGYPT TO LIVE THERE FOR A WHILE BECAUSE THE FAMINE WAS SEVERE."

GENESIS 12:10

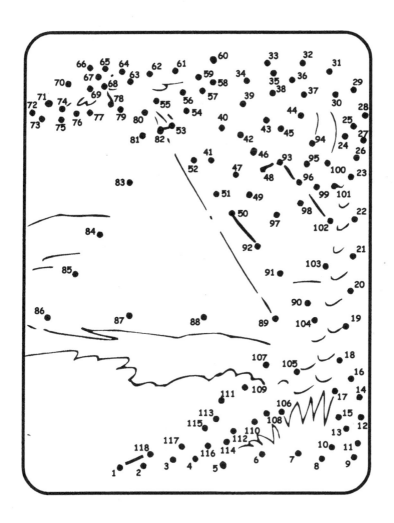

191

RIGHT OR WRONG

HAVE YOU EVER CHOSEN TO LIE BECAUSE YOU WERE AFRAID?

"AS HE WAS ABOUT TO ENTER EGYPT, HE SAID TO HIS WIFE SARAI, 'I KNOW WHAT A BEAUTIFUL WOMAN YOU ARE. WHEN THE EGYPTIANS SEE YOU, THEY WILL SAY, "THIS IS HIS WIFE." THEN THEY WILL KILL ME BUT WILL LET YOU LIVE. SAY YOU ARE MY SISTER, SO THAT I WILL BE TREATED WELL FOR YOUR SAKE AND MY LIFE WILL BE SPARED BECAUSE OF YOU.'"

GENESIS 12:11–13

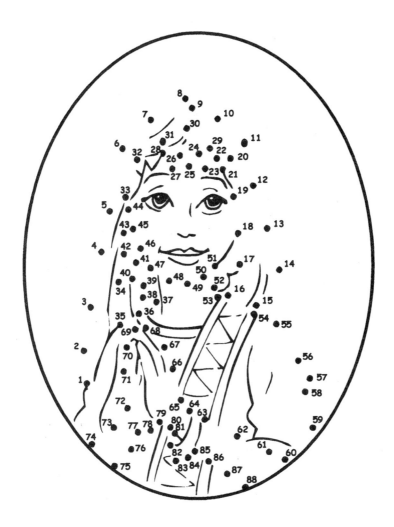

193

SAY WHAT?

HAVE YOU EVER ASKED SOMEONE ELSE TO LIE FOR YOU? HOW DOES THIS AFFECT THE OTHER PERSON?

"WHEN ABRAM CAME TO EGYPT, THE EGYPTIANS SAW THAT SHE WAS A VERY BEAUTIFUL WOMAN. AND WHEN PHARAOH'S OFFICIALS SAW HER, THEY PRAISED HER TO PHARAOH, AND SHE WAS TAKEN INTO HIS PALACE."

GENESIS 12:14–15

195

IT LOOKS PROFITABLE

IT LOOKS LIKE ABRAM PROFITED BY LYING ABOUT WHO SARAI WAS. BUT. . .*DOES* HE?

"HE TREATED ABRAM WELL FOR HER SAKE, AND ABRAM ACQUIRED SHEEP AND CATTLE, MALE AND FEMALE DONKEYS, MENSERVANTS AND MAIDSERVANTS, AND CAMELS."

GENESIS 12:16

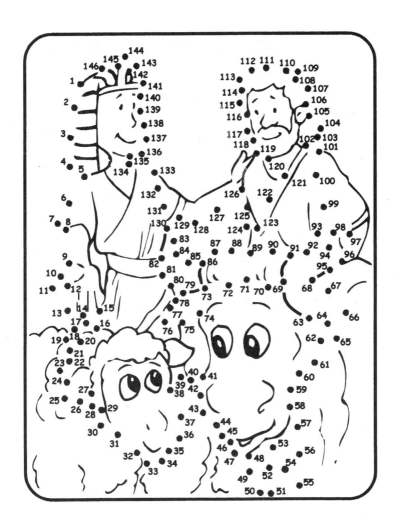

197

YOU CAN'T LIE TO GOD

YOU MAY BE ABLE TO LIE TO PEOPLE, BUT YOU CAN'T LIE TO GOD.

"BUT THE LORD INFLICTED SERIOUS DISEASES ON PHARAOH AND HIS HOUSEHOLD BECAUSE OF ABRAM'S WIFE SARAI."

GENESIS 12:17

199

THe TRUTH COMeS OUT

HAVE YOU EVER THOUGHT THAT YOUR CHOICE TO LIE AND ASK ANOTHER TO LIE FOR YOU CAN CAUSE *ANOTHER* HARM?

"SO PHARAOH SUMMONED ABRAM. 'WHAT HAVE YOU DONE TO ME?' HE SAID. 'WHY DIDN'T YOU TELL ME SHE WAS YOUR WIFE? WHY DID YOU SAY, "SHE IS MY SISTER," SO THAT I TOOK HER TO BE MY WIFE? NOW THEN, HERE IS YOUR WIFE. TAKE HER AND GO!'"

GENESIS 12:18–19

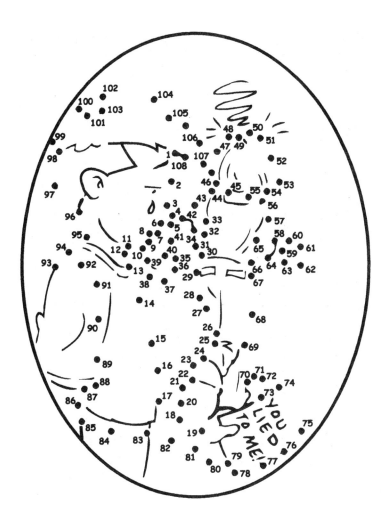

201

THINK, THINK, THINK

ABRAM DID AS GOD ASKED AND WENT TO SHECHEM. THE LORD APPEARED TO ABRAM AND PROMISED HIM THAT HE WOULD GIVE HIS OFFSPRING THE LAND.

BECAUSE OF A SHORTAGE OF FOOD, ABRAM WENT DOWN TO EGYPT TO LIVE. BUT. . .DID HE ASK *GOD* WHAT TO DO?

ABRAM TOOK MATTERS INTO HIS OWN HANDS, TRUSTING IN HIMSELF RATHER THAN GOD. HE ALSO ASKED HIS WIFE TO LIE AND TELL PHARAOH THAT SHE WAS NOT HIS WIFE, BUT HIS SISTER.

BECAUSE OF ABRAM'S LIE, EVERYONE SUFFERED. CAN YOU IMAGINE THE HURT THAT WAS CAUSED TO SARAI AND OTHERS BECAUSE ABRAM ACTED ON HIS OWN AND DID NOT TRUST IN GOD?

HAVE YOU EVER ASKED ANOTHER TO LIE FOR *YOU*? HAVE YOU EVER TRUSTED IN YOURSELF RATHER THAN GOD AND THE TRUTH? WHAT CAN YOU DO TO CORRECT A LIE? DO YOU THINK YOU CAN HIDE A LIE FROM GOD?

THINK, THINK, THINK!

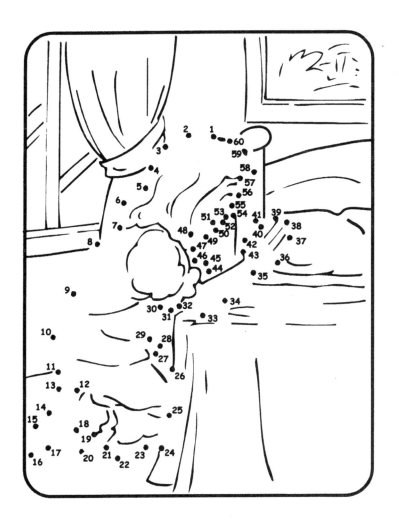

PACKING AGAIN

ABRAM ONCE AGAIN PACKED UP HIS FAMILY
AND HOUSEHOLD AND MOVED ON.

"SO ABRAM WENT UP FROM EGYPT TO
THE NEGEV, WITH HIS WIFE AND
EVERYTHING HE HAD, AND LOT WENT
WITH HIM. ABRAM HAD BECOME
VERY WEALTHY IN LIVESTOCK AND
IN SILVER AND GOLD."

GENESIS 13:1–2

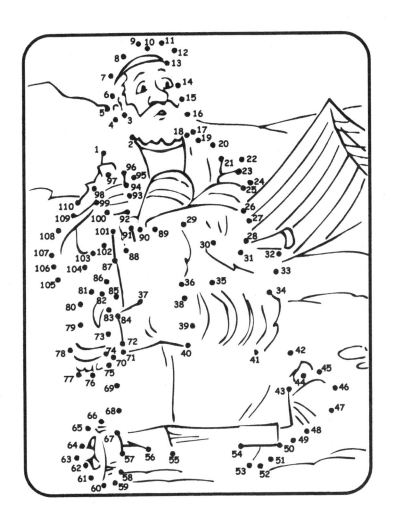

205

SECOND CHANCES

GOD CONTINUED TO SPEAK WITH ABRAM AND PROMISED HIM GREAT THINGS EVEN AFTER HE DID WHAT WAS WRONG. ARE THERE SECOND CHANCES WITH GOD?

"THE LORD SAID TO ABRAM AFTER LOT HAD PARTED FROM HIM, 'LIFT UP YOUR EYES FROM WHERE YOU ARE AND LOOK NORTH AND SOUTH, EAST AND WEST. ALL THE LAND THAT YOU SEE I WILL GIVE TO YOU AND YOUR OFFSPRING FOREVER.'"

GENESIS 13:14–15

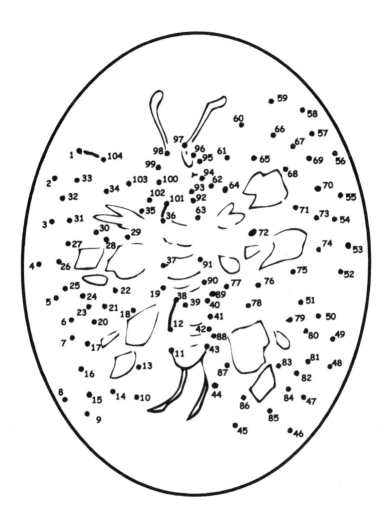

207

DUST OF THE EARTH

GOD SOMETIMES GIVES WHAT APPEAR TO BE *IMPOSSIBLE* PROMISES. BUT...ALL THINGS ARE POSSIBLE WITH GOD.

"'I WILL MAKE YOUR OFFSPRING LIKE THE DUST OF THE EARTH, SO THAT IF ANYONE COULD COUNT THE DUST, THEN YOUR OFFSPRING COULD BE COUNTED. GO, WALK THROUGH THE LENGTH AND BREADTH OF THE LAND, FOR I AM GIVING IT TO YOU.'"

GENESIS 13:16–17

209

PACKING YET AGAIN

WHY DID ABRAM BUILD AN ALTAR TO THE LORD? IS THIS ABRAM'S WAY OF REMEMBERING WHAT GOD HAS DONE FOR HIM AND HIS PROMISES TO HIM?

"SO ABRAM MOVED HIS TENTS AND WENT TO LIVE NEAR THE GREAT TREES OF MAMRE AT HEBRON, WHERE HE BUILT AN ALTAR TO THE LORD."

GENESIS 13:18

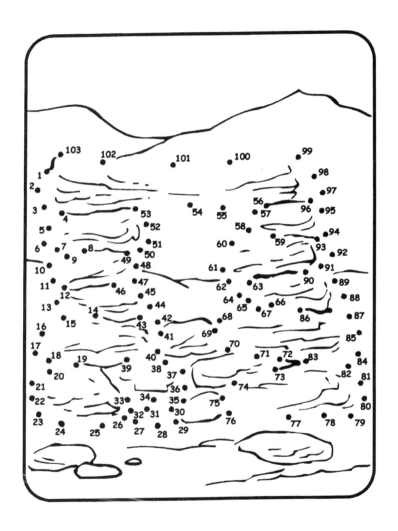

211

DO NOT BE AFRAID

HAVE YOU EVER WONDERED WHAT A *VISION* IS? IS IT A DREAM, OR IS IT LIKE WATCHING A MOVIE?

"AFTER THIS, THE WORD OF THE LORD CAME TO ABRAM IN A VISION: 'DO NOT BE AFRAID, ABRAM. I AM YOUR SHIELD, YOUR VERY GREAT REWARD.'"

GENESIS 15:1

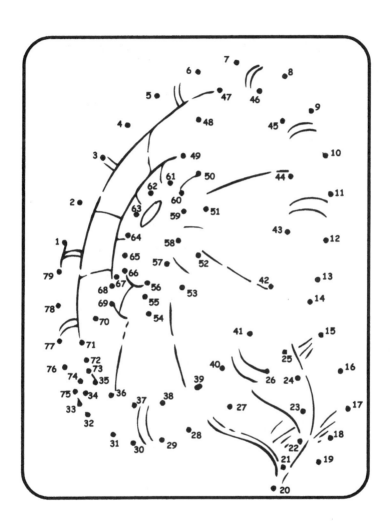

213

I HAVE NO CHILDREN

ABRAM LETS HIS NEED BE KNOWN TO GOD.

"BUT ABRAM SAID, 'O SOVEREIGN LORD, WHAT CAN YOU GIVE ME SINCE I REMAIN CHILDLESS AND THE ONE WHO WILL INHERIT MY ESTATE IS ELIEZER OF DAMASCUS?' AND ABRAM SAID, 'YOU HAVE GIVEN ME NO CHILDREN; SO A SERVANT IN MY HOUSEHOLD WILL BE MY HEIR.'"

GENESIS 15:2–3

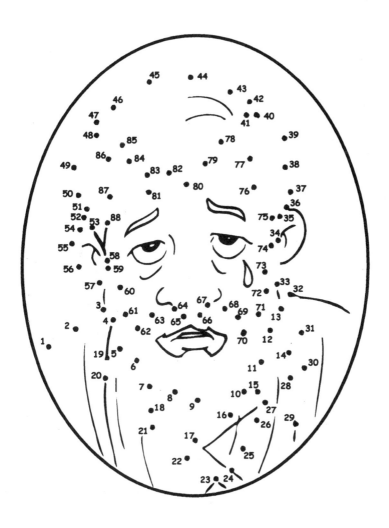

215

GOD UNDERSTANDS

GOD PROMISES THAT ABRAM WILL HAVE A SON.
DOES GOD EVER BREAK HIS PROMISES? WHAT
IS A PROMISE?

"THEN THE WORD OF THE LORD CAME
TO HIM: 'THIS MAN WILL NOT BE YOUR
HEIR, BUT A SON COMING FROM YOUR
OWN BODY WILL BE YOUR HEIR.' HE
TOOK HIM OUTSIDE AND SAID, 'LOOK
UP AT THE HEAVENS AND COUNT THE
STARS—IF INDEED YOU CAN COUNT
THEM.' THEN HE SAID TO HIM, 'SO
SHALL YOUR OFFSPRING BE.'"

GENESIS 15:4–5

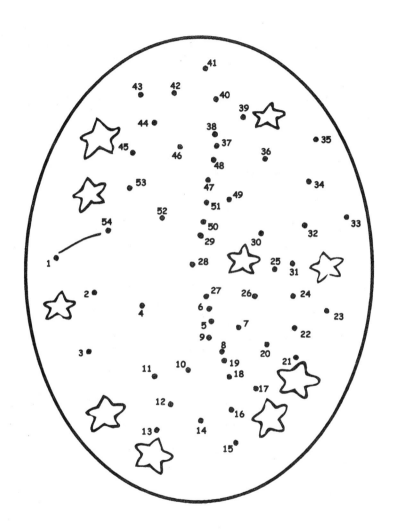

217

I BELIEVE YOU, LORD

WHAT DOES IT MEAN TO BELIEVE GOD? DO YOU HAVE A HARD TIME TAKING GOD AT HIS WORD?

"ABRAM BELIEVED THE LORD, AND HE CREDITED IT TO HIM AS RIGHTEOUSNESS."

GENESIS 15:6

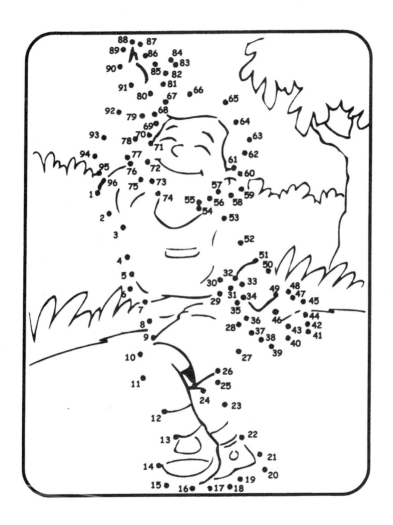

219

THINK, THINK, THINK

ONCE AGAIN GOD PROMISED ABRAM AND HIS OFFSPRING ALL THE LAND THAT HE SAW.

GOD KNEW THAT ABRAM WAS A PERSON THAT GAVE INTO FEAR. THE LORD TOLD HIM NOT TO BE AFRAID AND THAT *HE* WOULD PROTECT HIM.

ABRAM SEEMED TO FOCUS ON THE PROBLEM INSTEAD OF *HEARING* WHAT GOD SAID. HE SAID TO GOD THAT HE HAD GIVEN HIM NO CHILDREN, SO A SERVANT IN HIS HOUSEHOLD WOULD BE HIS HEIR. GOD REVEALED TO HIM THAT A SON WOULD BE BORN FROM HIS *OWN* BODY. ABRAM BELIEVED GOD, AND THIS BELIEF WAS GIVEN TO HIM AS RIGHTEOUSNESS.

HOW MANY TIMES DO YOU FOCUS ON THE PROBLEM AND NOT HEAR GOD'S SOLUTION FOR YOU? DO YOU TRUST GOD TO COME UP WITH A SOLUTION TO YOUR PROBLEMS? DO YOU BELIEVE THAT GOD CAN DO WHAT SEEMS TO BE IMPOSSIBLE?

THINK, THINK, THINK!

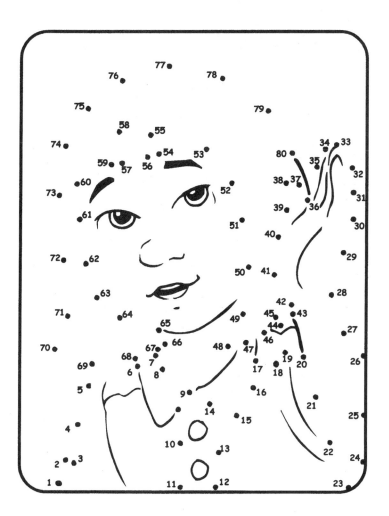

221

I AM THE LORD

WHY DO YOU THINK GOD TELLS ABRAM THAT HE IS THE LORD?

"HE ALSO SAID TO HIM, 'I AM THE LORD, WHO BROUGHT YOU OUT OF UR OF THE CHALDEANS TO GIVE YOU THIS LAND TO TAKE POSSESSION OF IT.'"

GENESIS 15:7

A COVENANT

WHAT DOES IT MEAN TO MAKE A COVENANT WITH SOMEONE?

"ON THAT DAY THE LORD MADE A COVENANT WITH ABRAM AND SAID, 'TO YOUR DESCENDANTS I GIVE THIS LAND, FROM THE RIVER OF EGYPT TO THE GREAT RIVER, THE EUPHRATES—THE LAND OF THE KENITES, KENIZZITES, KADMONITES, HITTITES, PERIZZITES, REPHAITES, AMORITES, CANAANITES, GIRGASHITES AND JEBUSITES.'"

GENESIS 15:18–21

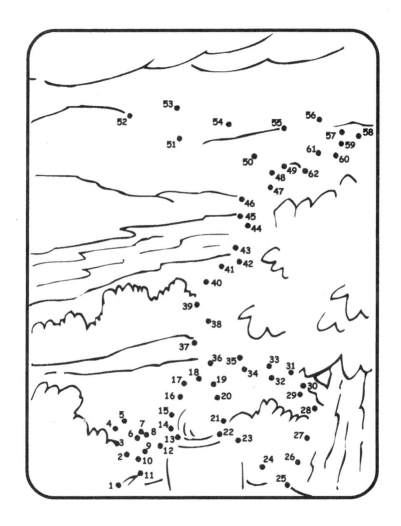

SARAI

IS THIS HOW GOD TOLD ABRAM HE WOULD HAVE CHILDREN?

"NOW SARAI, ABRAM'S WIFE, HAD BORNE HIM NO CHILDREN. BUT SHE HAD AN EGYPTIAN MAIDSERVANT NAMED HAGAR; SO SHE SAID TO ABRAM, 'THE LORD HAS KEPT ME FROM HAVING CHILDREN. GO, SLEEP WITH MY MAIDSERVANT; PERHAPS I CAN BUILD A FAMILY THROUGH HER.' ABRAM AGREED TO WHAT SARAI SAID."

GENESIS 16:1–2

227

BLAMING OTHERS

IS ABRAM AT FAULT, OR ARE BOTH ABRAM AND SARAI AT FAULT FOR THIS MISTAKE?

"WHEN SHE KNEW SHE WAS PREGNANT, SHE BEGAN TO DESPISE HER MISTRESS. THEN SARAI SAID TO ABRAM, 'YOU ARE RESPONSIBLE FOR THE WRONG I AM SUFFERING. I PUT MY SERVANT IN YOUR ARMS, AND NOW THAT SHE KNOWS SHE IS PREGNANT, SHE DESPISES ME. MAY THE LORD JUDGE BETWEEN YOU AND ME.'"

GENESIS 16:4–5

229

THINK, THINK, THINK

GOD TOLD ABRAM THAT HE WAS IN CONTROL AND NOT ABRAM. GOD MADE A PROMISE TO ABRAM NOT BASED ON *HIS* BEHAVIOR BUT ON GOD'S ACTIONS AND HIS WORD.

ABRAM'S WIFE WANTED CHILDREN AND TOOK MATTERS INTO HER OWN HANDS. WHEN SHE WENT TO ABRAM WITH HER SUGGESTION, ABRAM DID NOT SHARE WITH HER WHAT GOD HAD PROMISED HIM. RATHER THAN DO WHAT WAS RIGHT AND TELL SARAI TO TRUST AND WAIT ON GOD, ABRAM CHOSE TO TAKE HIS WIFE'S ADVICE. THEIR CHOICE NOT ONLY AFFECTED THEMSELVES BUT ALSO HAGAR, THE MAIDSERVANT, AND THE CHILD SHE NOW WAS CARRYING.

HAVE YOU EVER TAKEN THINGS INTO YOUR OWN HANDS TO HAVE YOUR NEEDS MET? HAVE YOU EVER THOUGHT OF HOW THIS COULD AFFECT OTHER PEOPLE?

THINK, THINK, THINK!

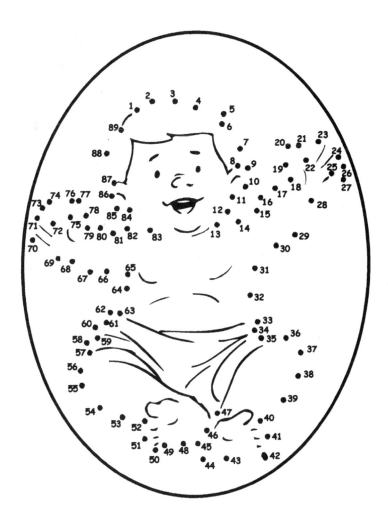

231

WALK BEFORE ME

WHAT DOES GOD MEAN BY SAYING, "I AM GOD ALMIGHTY"?

"WHEN ABRAM WAS NINETY-NINE YEARS OLD, THE LORD APPEARED TO HIM AND SAID, 'I AM GOD ALMIGHTY; WALK BEFORE ME AND BE BLAMELESS. I WILL CONFIRM MY COVENANT BETWEEN ME AND YOU AND WILL GREATLY INCREASE YOUR NUMBERS.'"

GENESIS 17:1–2

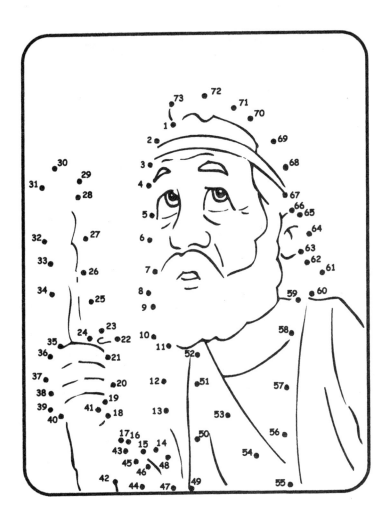

233

FATHER OF MANY

WHY DO YOU THINK GOD CHANGED ABRAM'S NAME TO ABRAHAM? WHAT WOULD BE GOD'S REASON FOR DOING THIS?

"ABRAM FELL FACEDOWN, AND GOD SAID TO HIM, 'AS FOR ME, THIS IS MY COVENANT WITH YOU: YOU WILL BE THE FATHER OF MANY NATIONS. NO LONGER WILL YOU BE CALLED ABRAM; YOUR NAME WILL BE ABRAHAM, FOR I HAVE MADE YOU A FATHER OF MANY NATIONS.'"

GENESIS 17:3–5

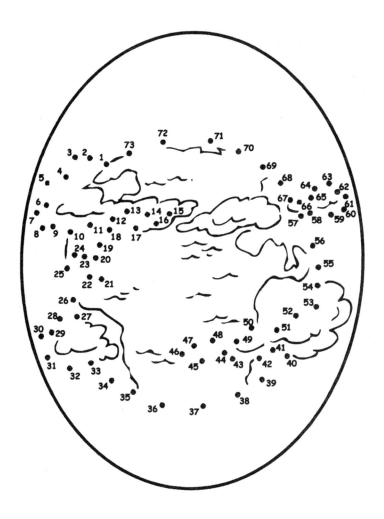

235

NEW NAMES

IN BIBLICAL TIMES, THE MEANING OF ONE'S NAME DESCRIBED *WHO* HE OR SHE WAS. HAVE YOU EVER TRIED TO FIND OUT WHAT YOUR NAME MEANS?

"GOD ALSO SAID TO ABRAHAM, 'AS FOR SARAI YOUR WIFE, YOU ARE NO LONGER TO CALL HER SARAI; HER NAME WILL BE SARAH. I WILL BLESS HER AND WILL SURELY GIVE YOU A SON BY HER. I WILL BLESS HER SO THAT SHE WILL BE THE MOTHER OF NATIONS; KINGS OF PEOPLES WILL COME FROM HER.'"

GENESIS 17:15–16

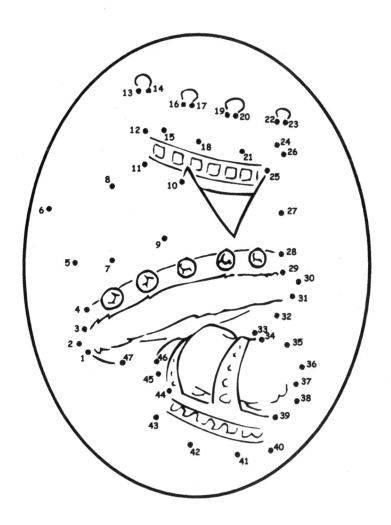

237

AT MY AGE?

EVEN IN ABRAHAM'S UNBELIEF, HE SHOWED RESPECT TO GOD WHEN QUESTIONING HIM.

"ABRAHAM FELL FACEDOWN; HE LAUGHED AND SAID TO HIMSELF, 'WILL A SON BE BORN TO A MAN A HUNDRED YEARS OLD? WILL SARAH BEAR A CHILD AT THE AGE OF NINETY?' AND ABRAHAM SAID TO GOD, 'IF ONLY ISHMAEL MIGHT LIVE UNDER YOUR BLESSING!'"

GENESIS 17:17–18

239

THINK, THINK, THINK

EVEN IN THE MIDST OF ABRAHAM'S MANY MISTAKES, GOD APPEARS AGAIN TO HIM AND CONFIRMS HIS PROMISE.

HE GIVES ABRAHAM A *NEW* NAME WHICH MEANS "THE FATHER OF MANY NATIONS." GOD NOT ONLY GAVE ABRAHAM A NEW NAME BUT ALSO TOLD HIM *WHAT IT MEANS.* DO YOU THINK HE DID THIS SO THAT EVERY TIME ABRAHAM HEARD HIS NAME HE WOULD BE REMINDED OF GOD'S PROMISE OF A SON?

EVEN THOUGH ABRAHAM LAUGHED AND QUESTIONED GOD, HE SHOWED RESPECT WITH THE GESTURE OF FALLING FACEDOWN. HE KNEW THAT HE WAS JUST A MAN, BUT GOD WAS ALMIGHTY AND ALL POWERFUL.

DO YOU EVER QUESTION GOD AND HIS PROMISES TO YOU? HOW WOULD YOU QUESTION GOD WITH AN ATTITUDE OF RESPECT?

THINK, THINK, THINK!

241

ISAAC

GOD NOT ONLY PROMISED ABRAHAM A SON BUT NAMED HIS SON FOR HIM. I WONDER WHAT THE NAME ISAAC MEANS?

"THEN GOD SAID, 'YES, BUT YOUR WIFE SARAH WILL BEAR YOU A SON, AND YOU WILL CALL HIM ISAAC. I WILL ESTABLISH MY COVENANT WITH HIM AS AN EVERLASTING COVENANT FOR HIS DESCENDANTS AFTER HIM.'"

GENESIS 17:19

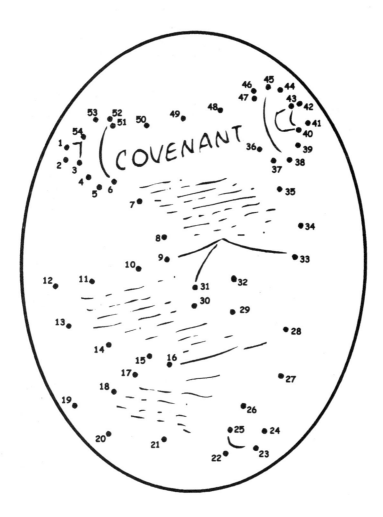

COVENANT

TREES OF MAMRE

ABRAHAM'S LIFE CERTAINLY INCLUDED SOME VERY UNUSUAL VISITORS!

"THE LORD APPEARED TO ABRAHAM NEAR THE GREAT TREES OF MAMRE WHILE HE WAS SITTING AT THE ENTRANCE TO HIS TENT IN THE HEAT OF THE DAY. ABRAHAM LOOKED UP AND SAW THREE MEN STANDING NEARBY. WHEN HE SAW THEM, HE HURRIED FROM THE ENTRANCE OF HIS TENT TO MEET THEM AND BOWED LOW TO THE GROUND."

GENESIS 18:1–2

245

FOUND FAVOR

DO YOU THINK ABRAHAM REALIZED AT FIRST JUST HOW SPECIAL THESE VISITORS WERE?

"HE SAID, 'IF I HAVE FOUND FAVOR IN YOUR EYES, MY LORD, DO NOT PASS YOUR SERVANT BY. LET A LITTLE WATER BE BROUGHT, AND THEN YOU MAY ALL WASH YOUR FEET AND REST UNDER THIS TREE. LET ME GET YOU SOMETHING TO EAT, SO YOU CAN BE REFRESHED AND THEN GO ON YOUR WAY—NOW THAT YOU HAVE COME TO YOUR SERVANT.'

'VERY WELL,' THEY ANSWERED, 'DO AS YOU SAY.'"

GENESIS 18:3–5

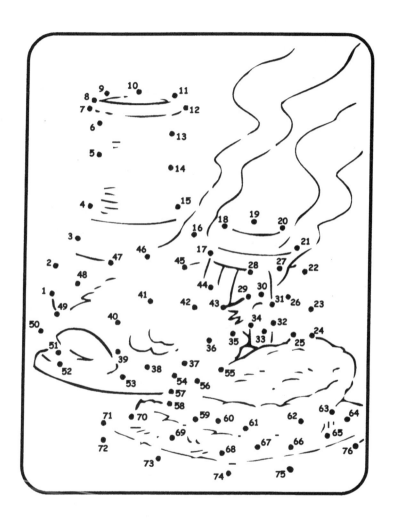

247

WHERE ARE YOU?

WHY WOULD THEY ASK ABRAHAM WHERE HIS WIFE WAS?

"'WHERE IS YOUR WIFE SARAH?' THEY ASKED HIM.

'THERE, IN THE TENT,' HE SAID."

GENESIS 18:9

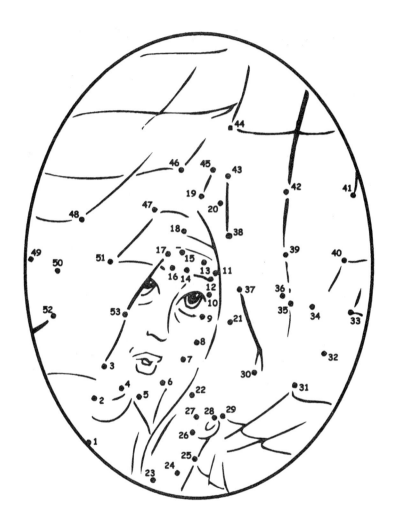

249

NEXT YEAR

GOD DOESN'T JUST TELL ABRAHAM THAT HE IS TO HAVE A SON, BUT *WHEN* HE WILL BE BORN.

"THEN THE LORD SAID, 'I WILL SURELY RETURN TO YOU ABOUT THIS TIME NEXT YEAR, AND SARAH YOUR WIFE WILL HAVE A SON.'"

GENESIS 18:10

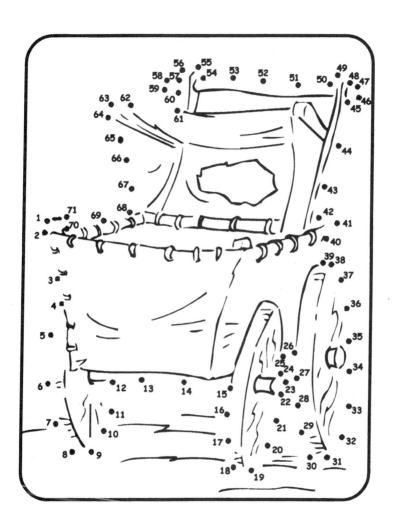

THINK, THINK, THINK

GOD TOLD ABRAHAM THAT HIS WIFE WOULD BEAR HIM A SON AND WOULD NAME HIM ISAAC.

HE PROMISED ABRAHAM THAT HE WOULD ESTABLISH HIS PROMISE WITH ABRAHAM'S SON— AN EVERLASTING PROMISE THAT WOULD BE FOR ALL HIS FAMILY.

WHEN THE LORD APPEARED TO ABRAHAM AGAIN, ABRAHAM ASKED THAT IF HE HAD FOUND FAVOR IN HIS EYES, HE WOULD LET HIM BRING FOOD TO EAT AND WATER TO WASH HIS FEET.

DID YOU NOTICE HOW MUCH ABRAHAM'S ATTITUDE CHANGED FROM WANTING SOMETHING FROM GOD TO WANTING TO GIVE OF HIMSELF TO GOD? DO YOU THINK GOD FOUND FAVOR WITH ABRAHAM BECAUSE HIS ATTITUDE CHANGED?

WHAT IS YOUR ATTITUDE LIKE WHEN YOU ARE TALKING TO GOD? DO YOU HAVE AN ATTITUDE OF ONLY WANTING FROM THE LORD OR OF GIVING TO THE LORD?

THINK, THINK, THINK!

253

WHEN I'M TIRED

DO YOU REALLY THINK THE LORD *DIDN'T* KNOW WHERE SARAH WAS, AND THAT SHE WAS LISTENING TO THEIR CONVERSATION?

"NOW SARAH WAS LISTENING AT THE ENTRANCE TO THE TENT, WHICH WAS BEHIND HIM. ABRAHAM AND SARAH WERE ALREADY OLD AND WELL ADVANCED IN YEARS, AND SARAH WAS PAST THE AGE OF CHILDBEARING. SO SARAH LAUGHED TO HERSELF AS SHE THOUGHT, 'AFTER I AM WORN OUT AND MY MASTER IS OLD, WILL I NOW HAVE THIS PLEASURE?'"

GENESIS 18:10–12

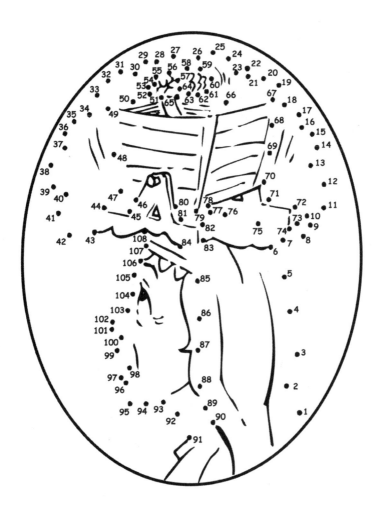

255

ANYTHING IS POSSIBLE

THERE ARE SO MANY THINGS IN OUR LIVES WE CANNOT CONTROL, BUT IS ANYTHING TOO HARD FOR THE *LORD?*

"THEN THE LORD SAID TO ABRAHAM, 'WHY DID SARAH LAUGH AND SAY, "WILL I REALLY HAVE A CHILD, NOW THAT I AM OLD?" IS ANYTHING TOO HARD FOR THE LORD? I WILL RETURN TO YOU AT THE APPOINTED TIME NEXT YEAR AND SARAH WILL HAVE A SON.'"

GENESIS 18:13–14

257

CHOOSING TO LIE

CAN YOU IMAGINE HOW *FOOLISH* IT IS TO LIE TO THE LORD?

"SARAH WAS AFRAID, SO SHE LIED AND SAID, 'I DID NOT LAUGH.'
　　BUT HE SAID, 'YES, YOU DID LAUGH.'"

GENESIS 18:15

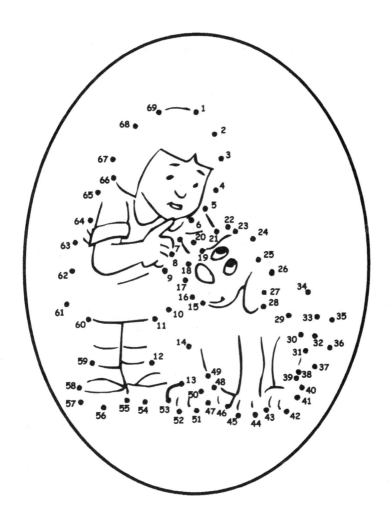

259

THINK, THINK, THINK

ABRAHAM'S WIFE, SARAH, WAS LISTENING IN ON ABRAHAM'S CONVERSATION WITH THE LORD.

WHEN SHE HEARD THE LORD SAY THAT SHE WOULD HAVE A SON, SHE LAUGHED TO HERSELF. WHEN SARAH WAS ASKED WHY SHE LAUGHED, RATHER THAN ADMIT WHAT SHE HAD DONE, SHE LIED BECAUSE SHE WAS AFRAID.

WAS SHE AFRAID BECAUSE SHE LAUGHED AT GOD OR BECAUSE SHE WAS EAVESDROPPING ON A PRIVATE CONVERSATION? DID SHE LAUGH BECAUSE SHE DID NOT BELIEVE GOD AND THOUGHT THIS TO BE AN IMPOSSIBLE TASK FOR HIM?

HAVE YOU EVER LAUGHED AT GOD BECAUSE YOU DID NOT BELIEVE WHAT HE PROMISED WAS POSSIBLE? DO YOU THINK IT STOPS GOD FROM FULFILLING HIS PROMISES?

THINK, THINK, THINK!

261

NOT AGAIN

ABRAHAM TRUSTS IN HIS *FEAR* ONCE AGAIN AND LETS THE KING BELIEVE SARAH IS HIS SISTER.

"NOW ABRAHAM MOVED ON FROM THERE INTO THE REGION OF THE NEGEV AND LIVED BETWEEN KADESH AND SHUR. FOR A WHILE HE STAYED IN GERAR, AND THERE ABRAHAM SAID OF HIS WIFE SARAH, 'SHE IS MY SISTER.' THEN ABIMELECH KING OF GERAR SENT FOR SARAH AND TOOK HER."

GENESIS 20:1–2

263

SHE'S MARRIED

HOW DO YOU THINK THIS LIE AFFECTED ABIMELECH'S VIEW OF ABRAHAM?

"BUT GOD CAME TO ABIMELECH IN A DREAM ONE NIGHT AND SAID TO HIM, 'YOU ARE AS GOOD AS DEAD BECAUSE OF THE WOMAN YOU HAVE TAKEN; SHE IS A MARRIED WOMAN.'"

GENESIS 20:3

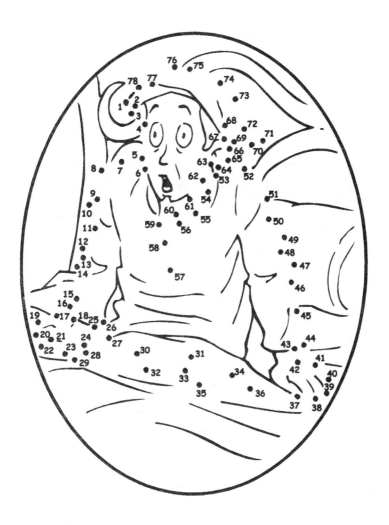

265

WHY?

HOW DO YOU DEAL WITH OTHERS' REACTIONS
WHEN YOU HAVE DONE SOMETHING WRONG?

"THEN ABIMELECH CALLED ABRAHAM IN
AND SAID, 'WHAT HAVE YOU DONE TO
US? HOW HAVE I WRONGED YOU THAT
YOU HAVE BROUGHT SUCH GREAT GUILT
UPON ME AND MY KINGDOM? YOU HAVE
DONE THINGS TO ME THAT SHOULD
NOT BE DONE.' AND ABIMELECH ASKED
ABRAHAM, 'WHAT WAS YOUR REASON
FOR DOING THIS?'"

GENESIS 20:9–10

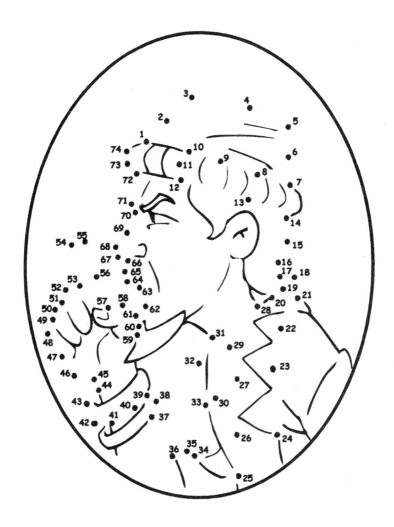

267

HALF-TRUTHS

PEOPLE HAVE A WAY OF TELLING THEMSELVES *ANYTHING* TO MAKE THEM FEEL BETTER.

"ABRAHAM REPLIED, 'I SAID TO MYSELF, "THERE IS SURELY NO FEAR OF GOD IN THIS PLACE, AND THEY WILL KILL ME BECAUSE OF MY WIFE." BESIDES, SHE REALLY IS MY SISTER, THE DAUGHTER OF MY FATHER THOUGH NOT OF MY MOTHER; AND SHE BECAME MY WIFE. AND WHEN GOD HAD ME WANDER FROM MY FATHER'S HOUSEHOLD, I SAID TO HER, "THIS IS HOW YOU CAN SHOW YOUR LOVE TO ME: EVERYWHERE WE GO, SAY OF ME, 'HE IS MY BROTHER.'"'"

GENESIS 20:11–13

THINK, THINK, THINK

YOU WOULD THINK AFTER ALL THAT HAD HAPPENED, ABRAHAM WOULD TRUST *GOD* AND NOT GIVE INTO HIS FEAR!

ABRAHAM WAS ONLY HUMAN, AND THE FEAR WAS MORE POWERFUL TO HIM THAN TRUSTING GOD. AGAIN ABRAHAM TOOK MATTERS INTO HIS OWN HANDS.

THE KING, NOT ABLE TO UNDERSTAND WHY ABRAHAM WOULD DO SUCH A THING, QUESTIONED HIM. ABRAHAM ADMITTED HE DID IT OUT OF FEAR FOR HIMSELF AND TELLS THE KING SARAH WAS ONLY DOING WHAT HE HAD ASKED OF HER.

ABRAHAM USED A HALF-TRUTH TO PROTECT HIMSELF. A HALF-TRUTH IS WHEN PART OF THE STORY IS TRUE BUT YOU LEAVE OUT SOME... *IMPORTANT* DETAILS.

HAVE YOU EVER TOLD A "HALF-TRUTH" BECAUSE YOU WERE AFRAID? WERE YOU TRUSTING IN YOURSELF OR GOD BY TELLING HALF-TRUTHS?

THINK, THINK, THINK!

271

NOT GUILTY

WHAT ABRAHAM ASKED SARAH TO DO WAS WRONG, AND ABIMELECH DECLARED HER INNOCENT.

"TO SARAH HE SAID, 'I AM GIVING YOUR BROTHER A THOUSAND SHEKELS OF SILVER. THIS IS TO COVER THE OFFENSE AGAINST YOU BEFORE ALL WHO ARE WITH YOU; YOU ARE COMPLETELY VINDICATED.'"

GENESIS 20:16

272

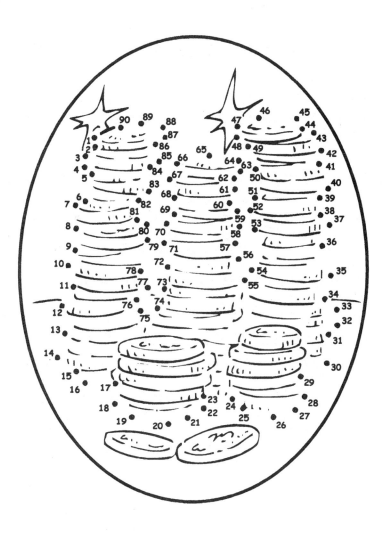

273

HEALED

WHY DO YOU THINK GOD CLOSED UP EVERY WOMB IN ABIMELECH'S HOUSEHOLD?

"THEN ABRAHAM PRAYED TO GOD, AND GOD HEALED ABIMELECH, HIS WIFE AND HIS SLAVE GIRLS SO THEY COULD HAVE CHILDREN AGAIN, FOR THE LORD HAD CLOSED UP EVERY WOMB IN ABIMELECH'S HOUSEHOLD BECAUSE OF ABRAHAM'S WIFE SARAH."

GENESIS 20:17-18

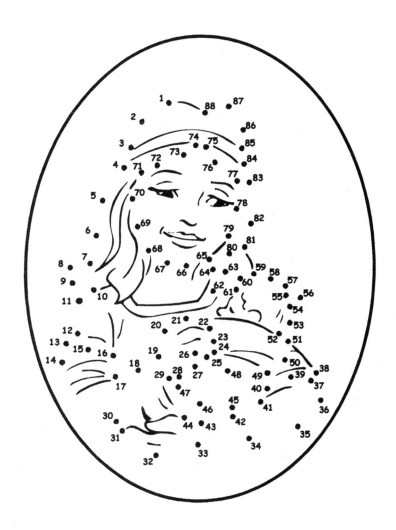

275

GOD'S FAITHULNESS

CAN YOU THINK OF TIMES WHEN GOD HAS SHOWN YOU HIS AWESOME FAITHFULNESS?

"NOW THE LORD WAS GRACIOUS TO SARAH AS HE HAD SAID, AND THE LORD DID FOR SARAH WHAT HE HAD PROMISED. SARAH BECAME PREGNANT AND BORE A SON TO ABRAHAM IN HIS OLD AGE, AT THE VERY TIME GOD HAD PROMISED HIM."

GENESIS 21:1–2

277

THINK, THINK, THINK

ABIMELECH WENT TO SARAH AND TOLD HER THAT HE GAVE ABRAHAM A THOUSAND SHEKELS OF SILVER TO COVER THE OFFENSE AGAINST HER. HE TOLD HER SHE WAS NOT GUILTY OF ANY WRONG.

WHILE SARAH WAS IN ABIMELECH'S HOUSE-HOLD, GOD STOPPED ANYONE FROM HAVING CHILDREN. ABRAHAM PRAYED TO GOD, AND GOD HEALED EVERY WOMB. ONCE ABRAHAM'S WRONG WAS CORRECTED, THE LORD DID FOR SARAH WHAT HE HAD PROMISED, AND SARAH BORE ABRAHAM A SON.

CAN YOU LEARN FROM ABRAHAM'S MISTAKE? HAVE YOU EVER DONE WRONG AND EXPECTED IN THE MIDST OF YOUR WRONG THAT GOD WOULD BLESS YOU?

IT TAKES COURAGE TO ADMIT TO YOUR WRONGS. EVEN THOUGH YOUR WRONGS DON'T CHANGE GOD'S PROMISES, HOW DO YOU THINK THEY STOP YOU FROM EXPERIENCING GOD'S PROMISES?

THINK, THINK, THINK!

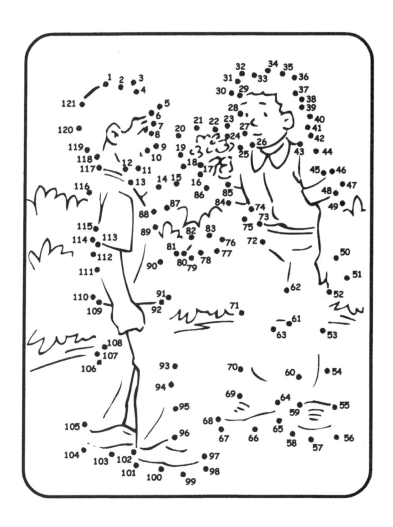

279

ISAAC

ABRAHAM NAMED HIS SON ISAAC, THE NAME GOD HAD GIVEN HIM FOR HIS SON.

"ABRAHAM GAVE THE NAME ISAAC TO THE SON SARAH BORE HIM. WHEN HIS SON ISAAC WAS EIGHT DAYS OLD, ABRAHAM CIRCUMCISED HIM, AS GOD COMMANDED HIM. ABRAHAM WAS A HUNDRED YEARS OLD WHEN HIS SON ISAAC WAS BORN TO HIM."

GENESIS 21:3–5

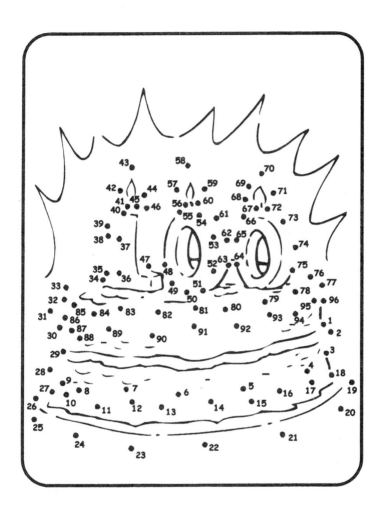

LAUGHTER

IMAGINE SARAH'S JOY AT GIVING BIRTH TO A SON IN HER OLD AGE!

"SARAH SAID, 'GOD HAS BROUGHT ME LAUGHTER, AND EVERYONE WHO HEARS ABOUT THIS WILL LAUGH WITH ME.' AND SHE ADDED, 'WHO WOULD HAVE SAID TO ABRAHAM THAT SARAH WOULD NURSE CHILDREN? YET I HAVE BORNE HIM A SON IN HIS OLD AGE.'"

GENESIS 21:6–7

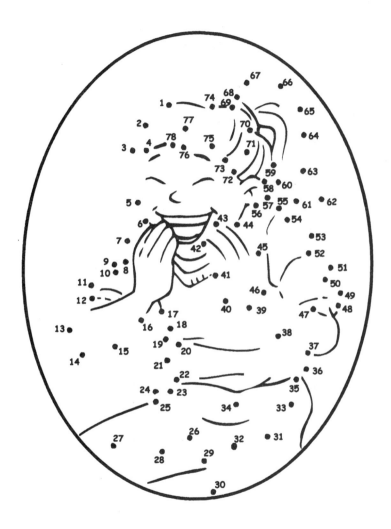

283

THINK, THINK, THINK

ABRAHAM NAMED HIS SON ISAAC, THE VERY NAME GOD HAD GIVEN HIM TO USE. SARAH WAS FILLED WITH JOY AT GIVING BIRTH IN HER OLD AGE.

ABRAHAM AND SARAH DID NOT DO EVERYTHING PERFECTLY—THEY MADE MANY MISTAKES WHICH WERE HURTFUL TO OTHERS. THE LORD ALLOWED NATURAL CONSEQUENCES OF THEIR WRONGS TO OCCUR.

WHY DO YOU THINK GOD ALLOWED THE NATURAL CONSEQUENCES OF THEIR CHOICES TO HAPPEN? DO YOU THINK THAT YOU CAN DO SOMETHING WRONG AND NEVER GET CAUGHT?

DO YOU THINK GOD WANTS YOU TO STAY IN YOUR WRONG CHOICES? WHY DO YOU THINK GOD WANTS YOU TO CORRECT YOUR WRONGS? DOES GOD STILL LOVE YOU WHEN YOU DO WRONG?

THINK, THINK, THINK!

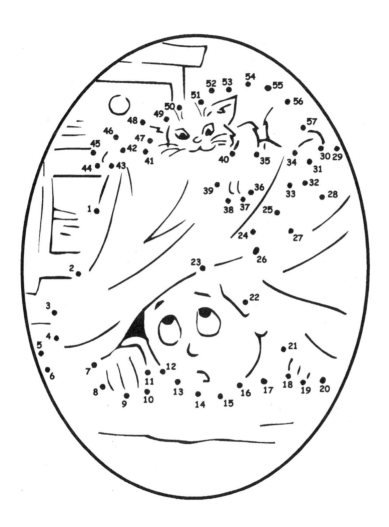

285

JEALOUSY

SARAH FELT THREATENED BY HAGAR AND HER SON AND TOOK MATTERS INTO HER OWN HANDS.

"BUT SARAH SAW THAT THE SON WHOM HAGAR THE EGYPTIAN HAD BORNE TO ABRAHAM WAS MOCKING, AND SHE SAID TO ABRAHAM, 'GET RID OF THAT SLAVE WOMAN AND HER SON, FOR THAT SLAVE WOMAN'S SON WILL NEVER SHARE IN THE INHERITANCE WITH MY SON ISAAC.'"

GENESIS 21:9–10

287

FRIGHTENED

ABRAHAM WAS BOTHERED BY WHAT SARAH HAD ASKED HIM TO DO AS IT CONCERNED HIS SON.

"THE MATTER DISTRESSED ABRAHAM GREATLY BECAUSE IT CONCERNED HIS SON. BUT GOD SAID TO HIM, 'DO NOT BE SO DISTRESSED ABOUT THE BOY AND YOUR MAIDSERVANT. LISTEN TO WHATEVER SARAH TELLS YOU, BECAUSE IT IS THROUGH ISAAC THAT YOUR OFFSPRING WILL BE RECKONED. I WILL MAKE THE SON OF THE MAIDSERVANT INTO A NATION ALSO, BECAUSE HE IS YOUR OFFSPRING.'"

GENESIS 21:11–13

289

HAGAR LEAVES

ABRAHAM TRUSTED THAT EVEN THOUGH HE DIDN'T LIKE SENDING HAGAR AWAY, GOD WOULD LOOK AFTER THEM BOTH AS HE HAD PROMISED.

"EARLY THE NEXT MORNING ABRAHAM TOOK SOME FOOD AND A SKIN OF WATER AND GAVE THEM TO HAGAR. HE SET THEM ON HER SHOULDERS AND THEN SENT HER OFF WITH THE BOY. SHE WENT ON HER WAY AND WANDERED IN THE DESERT OF BEERSHEBA."

GENESIS 21:14

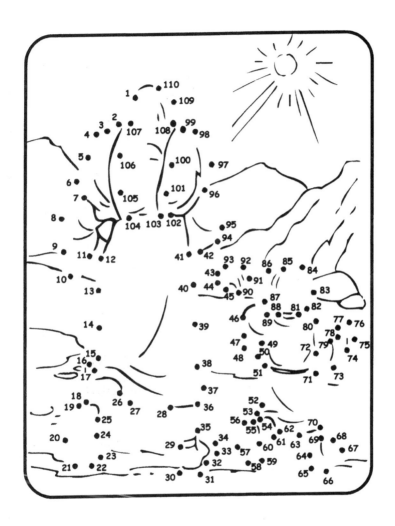

291

SHE CRIED

HAGAR THOUGHT SHE WOULD HAVE TO WATCH HER SON DIE.

"WHEN THE WATER IN THE SKIN WAS GONE, SHE PUT THE BOY UNDER ONE OF THE BUSHES. THEN SHE WENT OFF AND SAT DOWN NEARBY, ABOUT A BOW-SHOT AWAY, FOR SHE THOUGHT, 'I CANNOT WATCH THE BOY DIE.' AND AS SHE SAT THERE NEARBY, SHE BEGAN TO SOB."

GENESIS 21:15-16

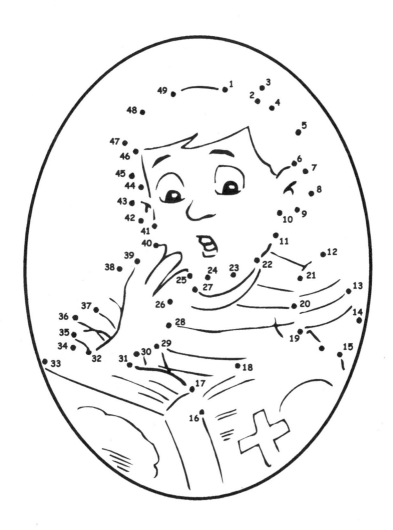

293

FEAR NOT

GOD HEARD THE BOY CRYING AND PROMISED HAGAR HE WOULD TAKE CARE OF HIM.

"GOD HEARD THE BOY CRYING, AND THE ANGEL OF GOD CALLED TO HAGAR FROM HEAVEN AND SAID TO HER, 'WHAT IS THE MATTER, HAGAR? DO NOT BE AFRAID; GOD HAS HEARD THE BOY CRYING AS HE LIES THERE. LIFT THE BOY UP AND TAKE HIM BY THE HAND, FOR I WILL MAKE HIM INTO A GREAT NATION.'"

GENESIS 21:17–18

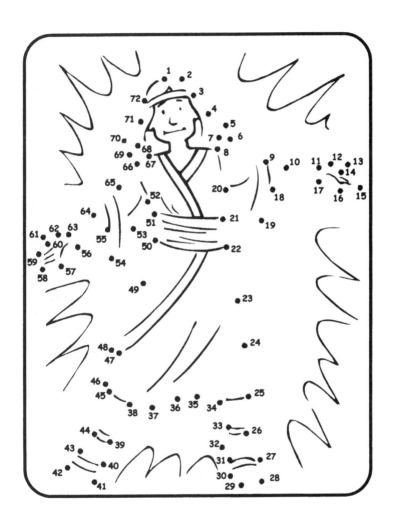

GOD PROVIDED

BECAUSE HAGAR WAS SO UPSET, SHE DID NOT SEE THE WELL UNTIL GOD OPENED HER EYES.

"THEN GOD OPENED HER EYES AND SHE SAW A WELL OF WATER. SO SHE WENT AND FILLED THE SKIN WITH WATER AND GAVE THE BOY A DRINK."

GENESIS 21:19

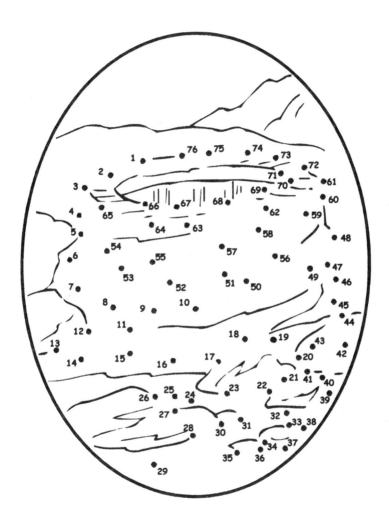

297

THINK, THINK, THINK

SARAH WAS JEALOUS OF HAGAR AND HER SON AND TOLD ABRAHAM TO GET RID OF THEM. GOD ASSURED HIM THAT HE WOULD EXTEND HIS PROMISE TO HAGAR'S SON.

WHEN HAGAR'S SUPPLIES HAD RUN OUT, SHE THOUGHT THAT THE BOY WOULD DIE, BUT GOD SPOKE WITH HER AND PROMISED THAT HE WOULD MAKE HER SON INTO A GREAT NATION. THEN GOD OPENED HAGAR'S EYES SO SHE COULD SEE THE WELL OF WATER.

MANY TIMES IN OUR LIVES WE WILL MAKE MISTAKES AND DO THINGS THAT ARE WRONG. GOD MAY NOT LIKE WHAT WE CHOOSE, BUT IT DOES NOT STOP HIM FROM LOVING US. GOD CAN USE OUR MISTAKES AND TURN THEM AROUND FOR GOOD WHEN WE ADMIT TO THEM AND TURN THEM OVER TO GOD.

IS THERE SOMETHING YOU HAVE DONE THAT IS WRONG? DO YOU THINK GOD CAN USE WHAT YOU HAVE DONE WRONG AND TURN IT AROUND FOR GOOD? WHAT DO YOU NEED TO DO?

THINK, THINK, THINK!

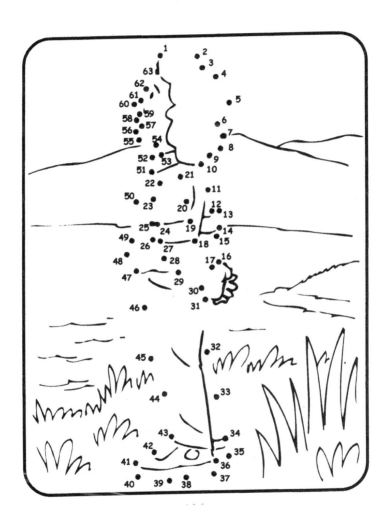

GOD TESTS ABRAHAM

WHAT WAS GOD TESTING ABRAHAM FOR?

"SOME TIME LATER GOD TESTED ABRAHAM. HE SAID TO HIM, 'ABRAHAM!' 'HERE I AM,' HE REPLIED."

GENESIS 22:1

301

eXCUSe Me, LORD?

DOES GOD REALLY GIVE YOU SOMETHING AND THEN TAKE IT AWAY?

"THEN GOD SAID, 'TAKE YOUR SON, YOUR ONLY SON, ISAAC, WHOM YOU LOVE, AND GO TO THE REGION OF MORIAH. SACRIFICE HIM THERE AS A BURNT OFFERING ON ONE OF THE MOUNTAINS I WILL TELL YOU ABOUT.'"

GENESIS 22:2

303

ALL RIGHT, LORD

COULD YOU IMAGINE WHAT ABRAHAM MUST HAVE BEEN FEELING EVEN THOUGH HE KNEW HE WAS DOING GOD'S WILL?

"EARLY THE NEXT MORNING ABRAHAM GOT UP AND SADDLED HIS DONKEY. HE TOOK WITH HIM TWO OF HIS SERVANTS AND HIS SON ISAAC. WHEN HE HAD CUT ENOUGH WOOD FOR THE BURNT OFFERING, HE SET OUT FOR THE PLACE GOD HAD TOLD HIM ABOUT."

GENESIS 22:3

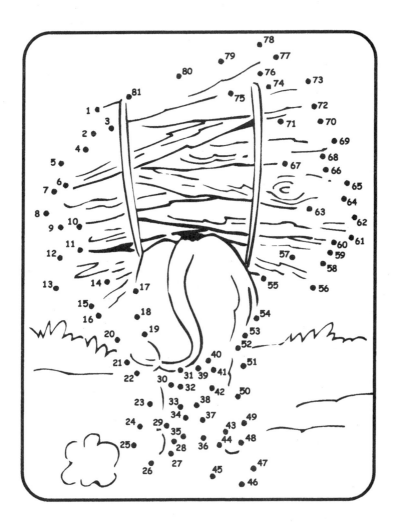

305

WE WILL COME BACK

LOOK CAREFULLY AT WHAT ABRAHAM SAID. HE DID NOT SAY, "I WILL COME BACK," BUT "*WE WILL COME BACK.*"

"ON THE THIRD DAY ABRAHAM LOOKED UP AND SAW THE PLACE IN THE DISTANCE. HE SAID TO HIS SERVANTS, 'STAY HERE WITH THE DONKEY WHILE I AND THE BOY GO OVER THERE. WE WILL WORSHIP AND THEN WE WILL COME BACK TO YOU.'"

GENESIS 22:4–5

FOLLOWING THROUGH

ABRAHAM WAS DOING AS GOD ASKED, IN SPITE OF WHAT HE MAY HAVE BEEN FEELING.

"ABRAHAM TOOK THE WOOD FOR THE BURNT OFFERING AND PLACED IT ON HIS SON ISAAC, AND HE HIMSELF CARRIED THE FIRE AND THE KNIFE."

GENESIS 22:6

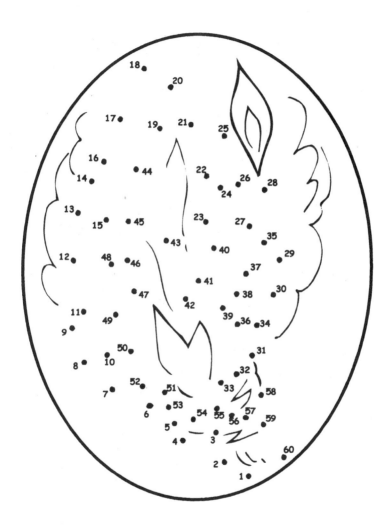

309

WHAT'S UP, DAD?

ISAAC BEGAN TO SEE THAT SOMETHING WAS NOT RIGHT.

"AS THE TWO OF THEM WENT ON TOGETHER, ISAAC SPOKE UP AND SAID TO HIS FATHER ABRAHAM, 'FATHER?'
'YES, MY SON?' ABRAHAM REPLIED.
'THE FIRE AND WOOD ARE HERE,' ISAAC SAID, 'BUT WHERE IS THE LAMB FOR THE BURNT OFFERING?'"

GENESIS 22:6–7

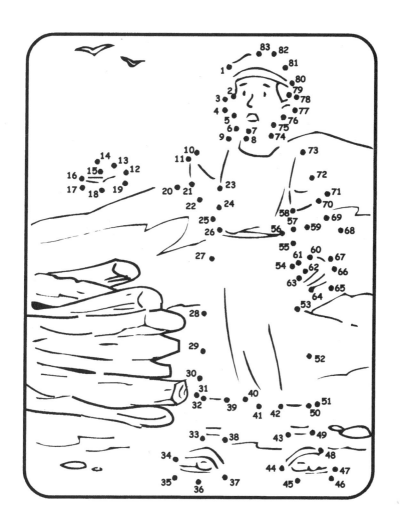

311

GOD WILL PROVIDE

ABRAHAM TOLD HIS SON ISAAC THAT GOD WOULD PROVIDE THE LAMB.

"ABRAHAM ANSWERED, 'GOD HIMSELF WILL PROVIDE THE LAMB FOR THE BURNT OFFERING, MY SON.' AND THE TWO OF THEM WENT ON TOGETHER."

GENESIS 22:8

313

ALL THE WAY

IT LOOKS LIKE GOD BROUGHT ABRAHAM RIGHT TO THE EDGE!

"WHEN THEY REACHED THE PLACE GOD HAD TOLD HIM ABOUT, ABRAHAM BUILT AN ALTAR THERE AND ARRANGED THE WOOD ON IT. HE BOUND HIS SON ISAAC AND LAID HIM ON THE ALTAR, ON TOP OF THE WOOD. THEN HE REACHED OUT HIS HAND AND TOOK THE KNIFE TO SLAY HIS SON."

GENESIS 22:9–10

315

THINK, THINK, THINK

GOD TESTED ABRAHAM, TELLING HIM TO SACRIFICE HIS SON ISAAC. ABRAHAM DID NOT TELL ANYONE ELSE ABOUT THIS—NOT EVEN ISAAC.

ABRAHAM TOLD ISAAC THAT GOD WOULD PROVIDE THE LAMB, BUT HE DID NOT SAY GOD WOULD PROVIDE A SACRIFICE. ABRAHAM KNEW WHAT GOD HAD PROMISED HIM ABOUT ISAAC.

CAN YOU IMAGINE WHAT BOTH ABRAHAM AND ISAAC WERE FEELING AND THINKING DURING THIS TIME? ABRAHAM TRUSTED IN GOD, AND ISAAC TRUSTED IN HIS FATHER, ABRAHAM.

CAN YOU REMEMBER A TIME WHEN GOD TESTED YOU? DID YOU DO AS GOD ASKED? WHAT WAS THE SCARIEST PART FOR YOU?

THINK, THINK, THINK!

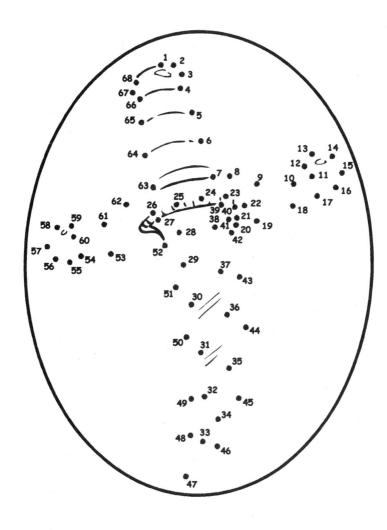

317

JUST IN TIME

ABRAHAM PASSED THE TEST BECAUSE HE WOULD NOT WITHHOLD HIS ONLY SON FROM GOD.

"BUT THE ANGEL OF THE LORD CALLED OUT TO HIM FROM HEAVEN, 'ABRAHAM! ABRAHAM!'

'HERE I AM,' HE REPLIED.

'DO NOT LAY A HAND ON THE BOY,' HE SAID. 'DO NOT DO ANYTHING TO HIM. NOW I KNOW THAT YOU FEAR GOD, BECAUSE YOU HAVE NOT WITHELD FROM ME YOUR SON, YOUR ONLY SON.'"

GENESIS 22:11-12

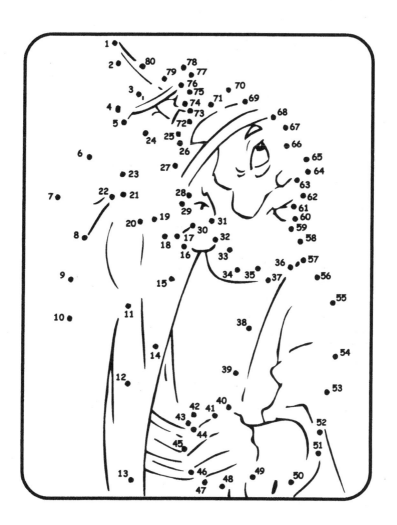

I WILL PROVIDE

CAN YOU IMAGINE THE RELIEF ABRAHAM WOULD HAVE FELT WHEN HE SAW THE RAM?

"ABRAHAM LOOKED UP AND THERE IN A THICKET HE SAW A RAM CAUGHT BY ITS HORNS. HE WENT OVER AND TOOK THE RAM AND SACRIFICED IT AS A BURNT OFFERING INSTEAD OF HIS SON. SO ABRAHAM CALLED THAT PLACE THE LORD WILL PROVIDE. AND TO THIS DAY IT IS SAID, 'ON THE MOUNTAIN OF THE LORD IT WILL BE PROVIDED.'"

GENESIS 22:13–14

321

ONE AND ONLY SON

WHAT COULD GOD MEAN WHEN HE SPOKE OF ALL NATIONS ON EARTH BEING BLESSED?

"THE ANGEL OF THE LORD CALLED TO ABRAHAM FROM HEAVEN A SECOND TIME AND SAID, 'I SWEAR BY MYSELF, DECLARES THE LORD, THAT BECAUSE YOU HAVE DONE THIS AND HAVE NOT WITHHELD YOUR SON, YOUR ONLY SON, I WILL SURELY BLESS YOU AND MAKE YOUR DESCENDANTS AS NUMEROUS AS THE STARS IN THE SKY AND AS THE SAND ON THE SEASHORE. YOUR DESCENDANTS WILL TAKE POSSESSION OF THE CITIES OF THEIR ENEMIES, AND THROUGH YOUR OFFSPRING ALL NATIONS ON EARTH WILL BE BLESSED, BECAUSE YOU HAVE OBEYED ME.'"

GENESIS 22:15–18

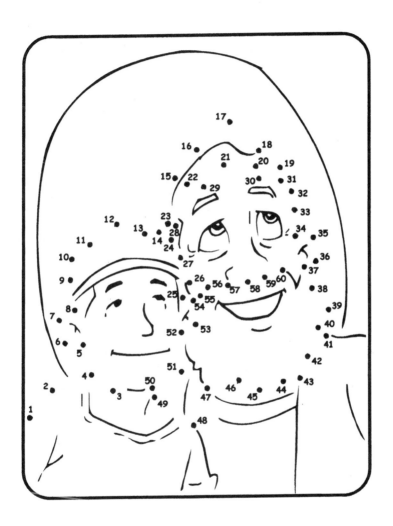

THINK, THINK, THINK

ABRAHAM WAS STOPPED BY GOD BEFORE ANY HARM CAME TO ISAAC. GOD KNEW BY ABRAHAM'S *ACTIONS* THAT HE PUT GOD FIRST, THAT HE TRUSTED IN GOD AND BELIEVED GOD AT HIS WORD.

GOD KNOWS EVERYTHING WE ARE THINKING AND FEELING. THERE IS NOTHING WE CAN HIDE FROM GOD. DID HE NEED TO HAVE ABRAHAM DO THIS TO PROVE HIS LOYALTY WHEN HE ALREADY KNEW ABRAHAM'S HEART? WAS THIS TEST FOR GOD OR WAS IT REALLY *FOR ABRAHAM?*

GOD KNEW THAT ABRAHAM NEEDED TO SEE FOR HIMSELF THAT HE LOVED GOD AND WOULD WITHHOLD NOTHING FROM HIM.

THROUGHOUT OUR LIVES, *WE* ARE GOING TO BE TESTED. THESE TESTS ARE NOT TO HARM US BUT TO HELP US GROW IN OUR FAITH AND TRUST IN GOD. IF GOD WERE TO ASK YOU TO SACRIFICE THE MOST IMPORTANT THING IN YOUR LIFE FOR HIM, WOULD YOU BE WILLING? WOULD YOU PASS THE TEST?

THINK, THINK, THINK!

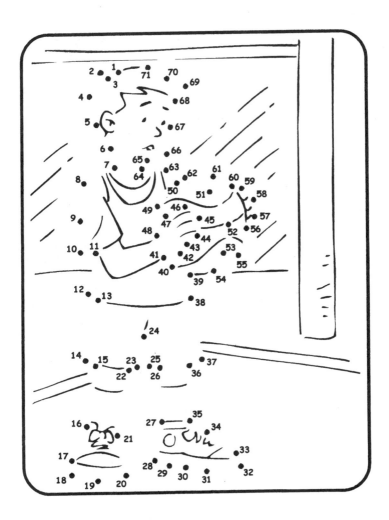

325

TEARS FOR SARAH

AFTER SO MANY YEARS TOGETHER, ABRAHAM HAD TO SAY GOOD-BYE TO HIS WIFE.

"SARAH LIVED TO BE A HUNDRED AND TWENTY-SEVEN YEARS OLD. SHE DIED AT KIRIATH ARBA (THAT IS, HEBRON) IN THE LAND OF CANAAN, AND ABRAHAM WENT TO MOURN FOR SARAH AND TO WEEP OVER HER."

GENESIS 23:1–2

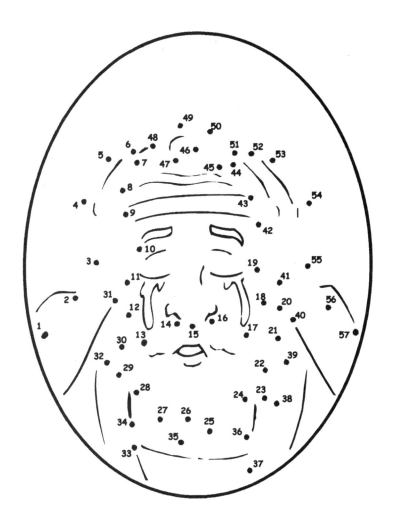

327

TIME TO REST

ABRAHAM NEEDED TO HAVE HIS OWN PLACE TO BURY HIS DEAD.

"THEN ABRAHAM ROSE FROM BESIDE HIS DEAD WIFE AND SPOKE TO THE HITTITES. HE SAID, 'I AM AN ALIEN AND A STRANGER AMONG YOU. SELL ME SOME PROPERTY FOR A BURIAL SITE HERE SO I CAN BURY MY DEAD.'"

GENESIS 23:3–4

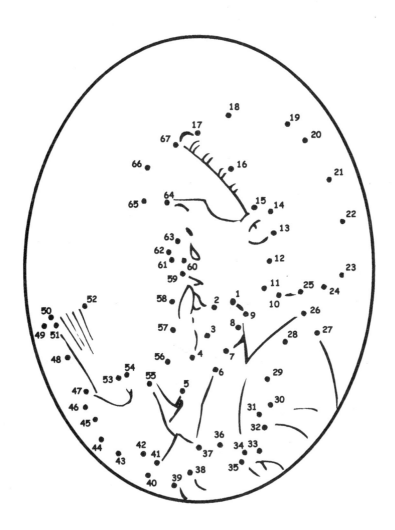

329

I AGREE

ABRAHAM HANDLED EVERYTHING FAIRLY AND ACCORDING TO WHAT EPHRON ASKED.

"ABRAHAM AGREED TO EPHRON'S TERMS AND WEIGHED OUT FOR HIM THE PRICE HE HAD NAMED IN THE HEARING OF THE HITTITES: FOUR HUNDRED SHEKELS OF SILVER, ACCORDING TO THE WEIGHT CURRENT AMONG THE MERCHANTS."

GENESIS 23:16

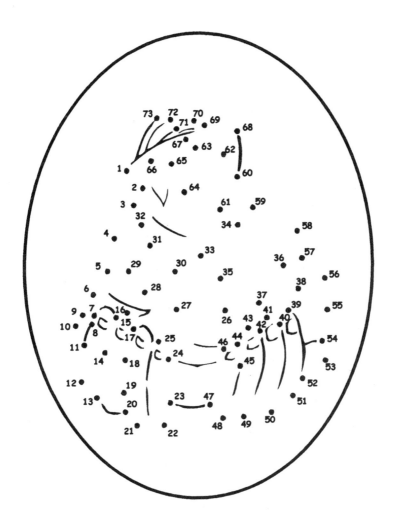

GRAVEYARD

WHY DO YOU THINK IT WAS SO IMPORTANT TO ABRAHAM TO BUY HIS OWN LAND FOR A BURIAL SITE?

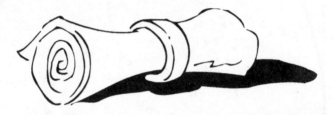

"AFTERWARD ABRAHAM BURIED HIS WIFE SARAH IN THE CAVE IN THE FIELD OF MACHPELAH NEAR MAMRE (WHICH IS AT HEBRON) IN THE LAND OF CANAAN. SO THE FIELD AND THE CAVE IN IT WERE DEEDED TO ABRAHAM BY THE HITTITES AS A BURIAL SITE."

GENESIS 23:19–20

THINK, THINK, THINK

ABRAHAM MADE MANY MISTAKES THROUGH-OUT HIS LIFE, BUT GOD'S PROMISE TO HIM NEVER CHANGED. GOD WAS ALWAYS FAITHFUL AND TRUE TO HIS WORD EVEN WHEN ABRAHAM WASN'T.

YOU CAN SEE THAT ABRAHAM STRUGGLED WITH FEAR. AFTER ISAAC WAS BORN AND GOD ASKED HIM TO SACRIFICE HIS ONLY SON, DO YOU SEE A DIFFERENT ABRAHAM? THROUGH HIS MISTAKES, MISTRUST, SELF-EFFORT, AND FEAR, ABRAHAM CAME TO KNOW NOT ONLY ABOUT HIS OWN HUMAN FRAILTIES BUT ALSO ABOUT GOD'S UNCONDITIONAL LOVE AND FAITHFULNESS.

ABRAHAM GREW UP AND LEARNED TO RELY AND TRUST IN GOD AND NOT HIMSELF.

WHEN YOU MAKE MISTAKES, DO YOU USE THEM TO GROW AND KNOW GOD THROUGH THEM? HOW CAN YOU USE YOUR MISTAKES TO GROW AND KNOW GOD?

THINK, THINK, THINK!

335

SWEAR BY THE LORD

ABRAHAM WANTED HIS SON TO HAVE A WIFE, BUT ONE FROM HIS OWN RELATIVES.

"ABRAHAM WAS NOW OLD AND WELL ADVANCED IN YEARS, AND THE LORD HAD BLESSED HIM IN EVERY WAY. HE SAID TO THE CHIEF SERVANT IN HIS HOUSEHOLD, THE ONE IN CHARGE OF ALL THAT HE HAD, 'PUT YOUR HAND UNDER MY THIGH. I WANT YOU TO SWEAR BY THE LORD, THE GOD OF HEAVEN AND THE GOD OF EARTH, THAT YOU WILL NOT GET A WIFE FOR MY SON FROM THE DAUGHTERS OF THE CANAANITES, AMONG WHOM I AM LIVING, BUT WILL GO TO MY COUNTRY AND MY OWN RELATIVES AND GET A WIFE FOR MY SON ISAAC.'"

GENESIS 24:1–4

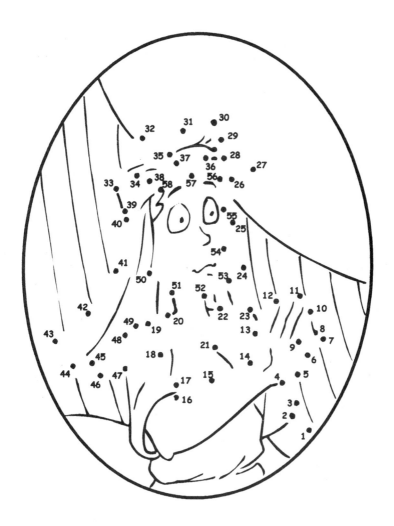

337

ON MY WAY

ABRAHAM'S SERVANT DID EXACTLY AS HE HAD ASKED OF HIM.

"THEN THE SERVANT TOOK TEN OF HIS MASTER'S CAMELS AND LEFT, TAKING WITH HIM ALL KINDS OF GOOD THINGS FROM HIS MASTER. HE SET OUT FOR ARAM NAHARAIM AND MADE HIS WAY TO THE TOWN OF NAHOR. HE HAD THE CAMELS KNEEL DOWN NEAR THE WELL OUTSIDE THE TOWN; IT WAS TOWARD EVENING, THE TIME THE WOMEN GO OUT TO DRAW WATER."

GENESIS 24:10–11

339

HELP ME, LORD

ABRAHAM'S SERVANT TURNED TO ABRAHAM'S GOD AND ASKED FOR HELP. WHY DO YOU THINK HE CALLED GOD "ABRAHAM'S GOD"?

"THEN HE PRAYED, 'O LORD, GOD OF MY MASTER ABRAHAM, GIVE ME SUCCESS TODAY, AND SHOW KINDNESS TO MY MASTER ABRAHAM. SEE, I AM STANDING BESIDE THIS SPRING, AND THE DAUGHTERS OF THE TOWNSPEOPLE ARE COMING OUT TO DRAW WATER. MAY IT BE THAT WHEN I SAY TO A GIRL, "PLEASE LET DOWN YOUR JAR THAT I MAY HAVE A DRINK," AND SHE SAYS, "DRINK, AND I'LL WATER YOUR CAMELS TOO"—LET HER BE THE ONE YOU HAVE CHOSEN FOR YOUR SERVANT ISAAC. BY THIS I WILL KNOW THAT YOU HAVE SHOWN KINDNESS TO MY MASTER.'"

GENESIS 24:12–14

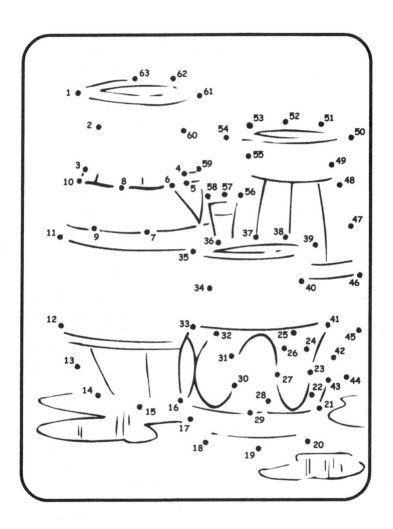

SUCCESS

THE SERVANT WATCHED REBEKAH CLOSELY TO SEE IF SHE WAS THE ONE FROM GOD.

"AFTER SHE HAD GIVEN HIM A DRINK, SHE SAID, 'I'LL DRAW WATER FOR YOUR CAMELS TOO, UNTIL THEY HAVE FINISHED DRINKING.' SO SHE QUICKLY EMPTIED HER JAR INTO THE TROUGH, RAN BACK TO THE WELL TO DRAW MORE WATER, AND DREW ENOUGH FOR ALL HIS CAMELS. WITHOUT SAYING A WORD, THE MAN WATCHED HER CLOSELY TO LEARN WHETHER OR NOT THE LORD HAD MADE HIS JOURNEY SUCCESSFUL."

GENESIS 24:19–21

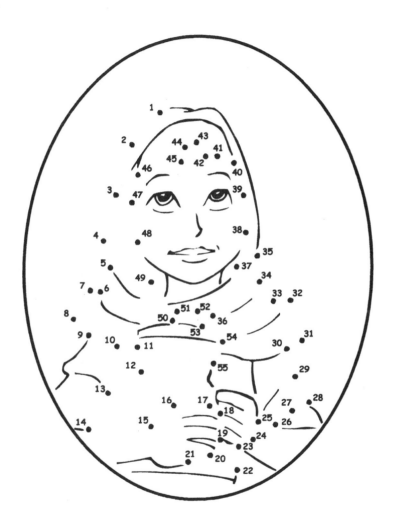

HE LOVED HER

ISAAC LISTENED TO THE SERVANT AND KNEW THIS WAS THE WIFE GOD HAD CHOSEN FOR HIM.

"THEN THE SERVANT TOLD ISAAC ALL HE HAD DONE. ISAAC BROUGHT HER INTO THE TENT OF HIS MOTHER SARAH, AND HE MARRIED REBEKAH. SO SHE BECAME HIS WIFE, AND HE LOVED HER; AND ISAAC WAS COMFORTED AFTER HIS MOTHER'S DEATH."

GENESIS 24:66–67

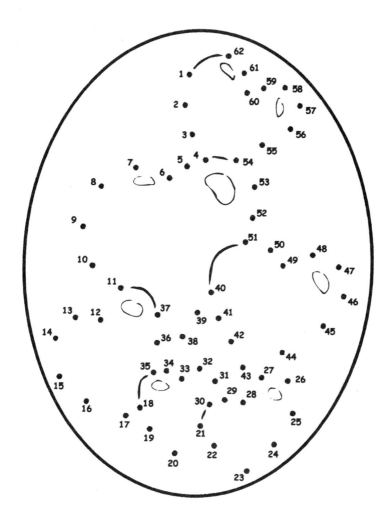

THINK, THINK, THINK

ABRAHAM KNEW HE WAS GETTING OLD, BUT BEFORE HE DIED HE WANTED TO KNOW THAT HIS SON ISAAC HAD A WIFE FROM THEIR OWN PEOPLE.

ABRAHAM'S SERVANT SWORE TO HIM TO DO AS HE ASKED. ABRAHAM'S SERVANT KNEW IN HIS MIND THAT THIS WAS A TASK THAT WAS *HUMANLY* IMPOSSIBLE. EVEN THOUGH HE DID NOT FOLLOW GOD HIMSELF, HE KNEW THAT ABRAHAM'S GOD WAS THE GOD OF THE IMPOSSIBLE.

HE PRAYED AND ASKED GOD TO HELP HIM. GOD DID JUST THAT, BRINGING TO THE SERVANT THE WIFE HE HAD CHOSEN FOR ISAAC.

IF SOMEONE WERE TO SEE *YOUR* RELATIONSHIP WITH GOD, WOULD HE SEE THAT YOU BELIEVE IN A GOD OF THE IMPOSSIBLE? DOES YOUR LIFE REFLECT GOD'S POWER AND LOVE OR YOUR *OWN* HUMAN EFFORTS AND LIMITATIONS?

THINK, THINK, THINK!

STARTING AGAIN

ONCE ABRAHAM HAD MADE SURE ISAAC WAS TAKEN CARE OF, HE TOOK ANOTHER WIFE.

"ABRAHAM TOOK ANOTHER WIFE, WHOSE NAME WAS KETURAH. SHE BORE HIM ZIMRAN, JOKSHAN, MEDAN, MIDIAN, ISHBAK AND SHUAH."

GENESIS 25:1–2

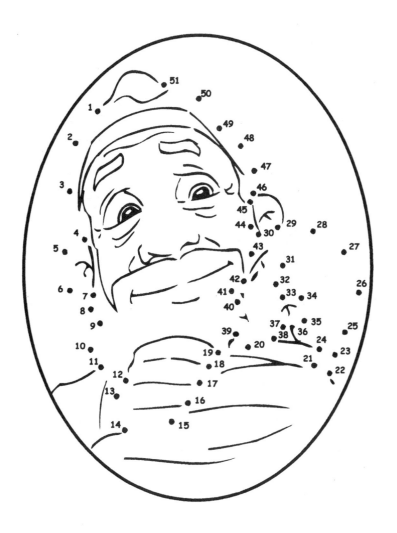

349

HE GAVE TO ALL

ABRAHAM MADE SURE THAT HE GAVE TO ALL HIS CHILDREN SO THAT THERE WOULD BE NO ARGUING OR JEALOUSY BETWEEN THEM.

"ABRAHAM LEFT EVERYTHING HE OWNED TO ISAAC. BUT WHILE HE WAS STILL LIVING, HE GAVE GIFTS TO THE SONS OF HIS CONCUBINES AND SENT THEM AWAY FROM HIS SON ISAAC TO THE LAND OF THE EAST."

GENESIS 25:5–6

MY TIME HAS COME

THE RECORD OF ABRAHAM'S LIFE TEACHES US SO MUCH. HIS LIFE IS FULL OF MANY EXPERIENCES THAT WE CAN LEARN FROM.

"ALTOGETHER, ABRAHAM LIVED A HUNDRED AND SEVENTY-FIVE YEARS. THEN ABRAHAM BREATHED HIS LAST AND DIED AT A GOOD OLD AGE, AN OLD MAN AND FULL OF YEARS; AND HE WAS GATHERED TO HIS PEOPLE."

GENESIS 25:7–8

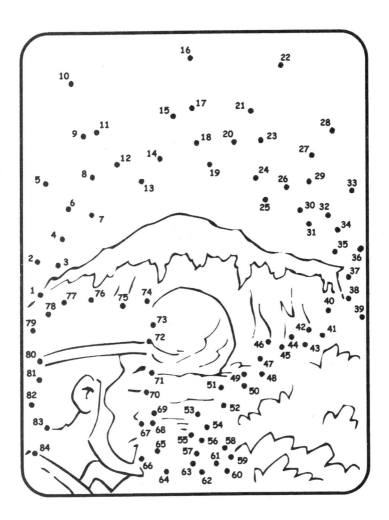

353

BOTH SONS

WHEN ABRAHAM WAS LAID TO REST, BOTH ISAAC AND ISHMAEL JOINED TOGETHER TO HONOR THEIR FATHER.

"HIS SONS ISAAC AND ISHMAEL BURIED HIM IN THE CAVE OF MACHPELAH NEAR MAMRE, IN THE FIELD OF EPHRON SON OF ZOHAR THE HITTITE, THE FIELD ABRAHAM HAD BOUGHT FROM THE HITTITES. THERE ABRAHAM WAS BURIED WITH HIS WIFE SARAH."

GENESIS 25:9–10

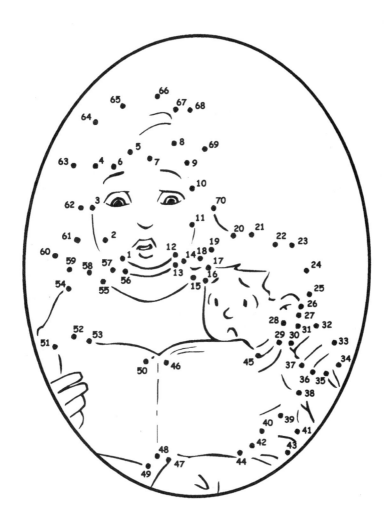

355

THINK, THINK, THINK

"BY FAITH ABRAHAM, WHEN GOD TESTED HIM, OFFERED ISAAC AS A SACRIFICE. HE WHO HAD RECEIVED THE PROMISES WAS ABOUT TO SACRIFICE HIS ONE AND ONLY SON, EVEN THOUGH GOD HAD SAID TO HIM, 'IT IS THROUGH ISAAC THAT YOUR OFFSPRING WILL BE RECKONED.' ABRAHAM REASONED THAT GOD COULD RAISE THE DEAD, AND FIGURATIVELY SPEAKING, HE DID RECEIVE ISAAC BACK FROM DEATH."

HEBREWS 11:17–19

LOOKING AT ABRAHAM'S LIFE, WE SEE THAT HE WAS JUST A MAN WHO MADE MISTAKES AND LEARNED TO TRUST GOD THROUGH THEM. WE ALSO SEE GOD'S PATIENCE, LOVE, AND FAITHFULNESS WITH ABRAHAM.

ABRAHAM IS THOUGHT OF AS A MAN OF GREAT FAITH BECAUSE HE LEARNED TO BELIEVE GOD AND TRUST HIM TO DO AS HE SAID HE WOULD. BELIEVING GOD IS NOT ENOUGH; YOUR BELIEF MUST HAVE *ACTION* BEHIND IT.

DO YOU BELIEVE AND TRUST GOD? HOW?

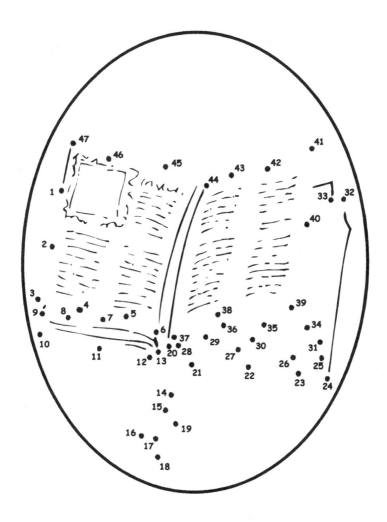

357

THINK, THINK, THINK

"YOU SEE THAT HIS FAITH AND HIS ACTIONS WERE WORKING TOGETHER, AND HIS FAITH WAS MADE COMPLETE BY WHAT HE DID. AND THE SCRIPTURE WAS FULFILLED THAT SAYS, 'ABRAHAM BELIEVED GOD, AND IT WAS CREDITED TO HIM AS RIGHTEOUSNESS,' AND HE WAS CALLED GOD'S FRIEND. YOU SEE THAT A PERSON IS JUSTIFIED BY WHAT HE DOES AND NOT BY FAITH ALONE."

JAMES 2:22–24

BEING GOD'S FRIEND IS AN HONOR. HOW DOES ONE BECOME GOD'S FRIEND? IS IT BY BEING A GOOD PERSON? IS IT BY WHO *YOU* ARE?

OR IS IT BY BEING WILLING TO BELIEVE GOD AT HIS WORD AND PUTTING YOUR TRUST IN *HIM*?

YOU HAVE TO HAVE ACTION BEHIND YOUR BELIEF. YOUR *ACTIONS* ARE THE PROOF THAT YOU BELIEVE AND ARE WILLING TO TRUST GOD TO DO AS HE PROMISES. HOW ARE YOU SHOWING GOD THAT YOU BELIEVE HIM?

ARE YOU WILLING TO PUT "FEET TO YOUR FAITH"?

JESUS

YOU'VE READ ABOUT A GREAT MAN WHO HAD A GREAT FAITH. BUT HOW DO *YOU* HAVE THAT KIND OF FAITH? DO YOU THINK YOU CAN HAVE THAT KIND OF FAITH? NOT BY YOUR OWN EFFORT—BUT THERE IS *ONE* WHO CAN DO IT THROUGH YOU! ASK JESUS AND HE WILL SHOW YOU HOW AS HE LIVES HIS LIFE IN YOU.

"LET US FIX OUR EYES ON JESUS, THE AUTHOR AND PERFECTER OF OUR FAITH, WHO FOR THE JOY SET BEFORE HIM ENDURED THE CROSS, SCORNING ITS SHAME, AND SAT DOWN AT THE RIGHT HAND OF THE THRONE OF GOD."

HEBREWS 12:2

361

PG. 7

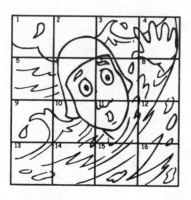

H O R S E S

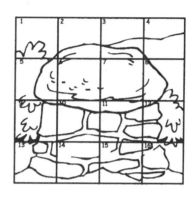

PG. 29

PG. 31

<u>S</u> <u>H</u> <u>E</u> <u>E</u> <u>P</u>

PG. 35

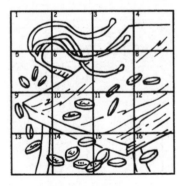

PG. 37

PG. 41

PG. 43

PG. 47

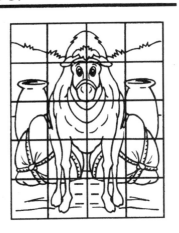

C O W

L I O N

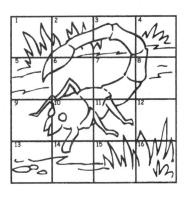

PG. 71

PG. 77

<u>D</u> <u>O</u> <u>G</u>

PG. 79

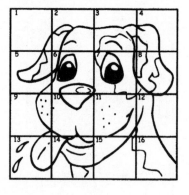

S N A K E

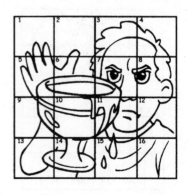

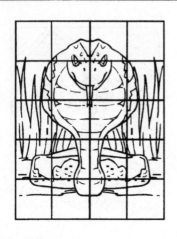

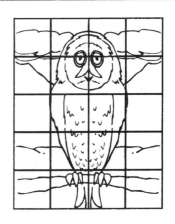

<u>O</u> <u>W</u> <u>L</u>

PG. 111

PG. 113

PG. 117

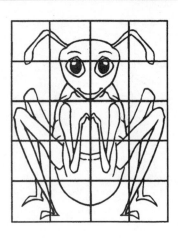

E A G L E

PG. 135

PG. 137

PG. 139

B E A R

PG. 151

PG. 153

F I S H

PG. 155

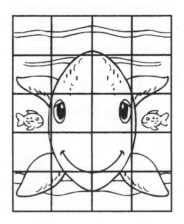

PG. 161

PG. 165

B I R D

PG. 167

PG. 171

If you enjoyed **Bible Picture Fun**
check out these other great Super Bible activity books!

Super Bible Trivia
for Kids
978-1-60260-393-6

Super Bible Activities
for Kids
978-1-60260-394-3

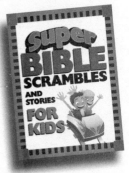

Super Bible Scrambles
and Stories for Kids
978-1-60260-396-7

Hours of Bible-based entertainment
for kids ages 8 to 12.

384 pages each / 5" x 6½" / Paperback

Available wherever Christian books are sold.